PAN AFRICAN LANGUAGE SYSTEMS
EBONICS & AFRICAN ORAL HERITAGE

KATHERINE J. HARRIS

Katherine J. Harris
Pan African Language Systems
Ebonics & African Oral Heritage

First published in English by
Karnak House
300 Westbourne Park Road
London W11 1EH
UK

Tel: +44 207.243.3620
Email: karnakhouse@aol.com
Website: karnakhouse.co.uk

ISBN ISBN 1 872596 07 X

CONTENTS

Acknowledgement

Chapter I
    EBONICS: THE CONTROVERSY   6
    Duality: African & African American Identity   7
    The Number Of African Languages & Classification   15

Chapter II
    AFRICAN LANGUAGES: TERMS, CREOLE, NAMES,   27
    GRAMMAR & VOCABULARY
    Geechee, Guichee, Gullah & Creole Languages   28
    Names   31
    Place Names   41
    African Grammatical Constructions   43
    Folklore   44

Chapter III -
    RAP, HIP HOP, GAMES, OTHER AFRICANISMS & EBONICS   47
    What is African About Rap & Hip Hop?   48
    Current Issues – Are Rap & Hip Hop The Same?   52
    Current Issue: Is Hip Hop African?   53
    Analysis & Examples Of Rap   55
    The Griot & Rap   57
    Themes, Form & Lexical Structure   61
    The Praise Song   64
    Women & Rap   73
    Story Telling, Tongue Twisters & Song Games   78
    Song Games   81
    English & African Speech   83
    African Words & Phrases   89
    Conclusion   91
    Amelia's Song   93

Notes & References   95
Bibliography   125
Index   141

ACKNOWLEDGEMENTS

Thank you to Professor Gloria Emeagwali for encouraging me to write the essay on Pan African Languages and Ebonics. Thank you to Dr. Amon Saba Saakana and Karnak for your interest in that essay and providing me with the opportunity to publish this volume. Thank you to my family especially my parents, wonderful Malik Sei, extended family and friends who have inspired me.

Gye Nyame!

CHAPTER 1

EBONICS, THE CONTROVERSY & BACKGROUND

In millennium 2000, debate continues on the Oakland Unified School District's (OUSD) 'Ebonics' resolution, specifically, "Pan-African Communication Behaviors."[1] The OUSD initiated the resolution as a linguistic tool to teach English skills. The December 1996 proposal was a local matter, but across the nation, educators and parents, most predictably, responded quickly – some with support and others with skepticism. But religious personalities, journalists and political officials joined the debate as well.[2]

The School Board explained its primary goal to enhance student learning, building on the linguistic communication systems that connected their speech patterns to African construction and sounds. Challengers insisted that Ebonics was another device to encourage academic mediocrity among African American students. During the passing months, the derisive comments and cartoons subsided. But the publication of Theresa Perry and Lisa Delpit's *The Real Ebonics Debate: Power Language, and the Education of African American Children* continued the discourse on issues of power, language, and identity of African-American children.[3]

Fig. 1: John Rickford, specialist in African American vernacular language.

While these themes are central to discussions of African American speech, *Pan African Language Systems Ebonics and African Oral Heritage* highlights grammar, vocabulary, names and other Africanisms which connect African American speech to Africa. This research examines the binary categories of linguistics to differentiate the synchronic aspects of African grammar, syntax and vocabulary that remained unchanged and the diachronic linguistic phrases that did change in the African American community. This book moves beyond the binary framework, however. It identifies the linguistic forms that blended to produce a unique syncretic Pan African language heritage.

DUALITY: AFRICAN & AFRICAN AMERICAN IDENTITY

A duality has shaped the experience of the descendants of Africans who arrived as captives in the Americas.[4] On one level, by emphasizing enhancement of African American students' English skills, the Oakland Unified School District (OUSD) has pointed to the quest for academic literacy viewed as a way out of socio-economic deprivation. On the second level, the resolution has accented a need for historical literacy by identifying the languages of West Africa and the Niger-Congo Rivers' confluence as the ancestral 'historical and cultural base' of African American speech in the 1990s.

The Ebonics debates, however, have brought to the forefront questions regarding the clear distinctions in such oral communication forms as slang, dialect and language. Slang is generally used to describe words in various languages that are idiomatic, colloquial, playful, and metaphorical and some-times socially taboo. Dialects, according to some linguists, are parts of a par-ticular language family. Refining the definitions of dialect and language, European linguist Ferdinand De Saussure contended that language has an individual and social aspect with an established system that is in a constant state of evolution. Language can be conceptualized as thought organized in sound. Between languages and dialects there is a difference of quality not nature. Languages differing only slightly are called dialects De Saussure explained. Other linguists insist that the distinction between "dialects" and "languages" is based on social and political grounds rather than purely lin-guistic ones.[5]

Disputes are likely to persist among educators over rigid categorization of Ebonics as slang, a dialect or language. The choice of the term Ebonics is another source of contention. One might ask why choose the term "Ebonics," composed of "ebony" which is Ancient Egyptian and "phonics" which is Greek?[6] Though "Ebonics" has been translated literally as "Black Sounds," the use of a Kemetic/Greco-Latin expression does not seem so incongruous when trying to connect African American speech to African lin-guistic bases. Also, there exist varieties of accents, slang, and vernacular rather than a uniform pattern of speech shared nationwide by African Americans.

The core issue of redressing scholastic inequities must not be lost howev-er. The 1990s debate on segregation in public educational institutions and unequal distribution of public finances for predominantly black facilities dates from the 1780s. African American families founded schools for their children in New York City during the 1780s and 1800s when it became appar-ent that the local government was reluctant to provide educational access.[7] Boston schools had often been segregated and unequal in terms of resources since 1798. The busing crisis in the 1980s briefly highlighted this pattern.[8] African American parents in Hartford, Connecticut sought legal remedies to educational inequities in the 1990s. However their efforts emerged from those begun by 19th century black parents. They organized Hartford's

North African School and South African School.[9]

The Oakland School Board's initiative calls attention to such longstanding issues of educational inequality which persist in the 1990s. In an attempt to enhance educational development of African American students, therefore, the Oakland School Board developed a resolution to use "Ebonics" or "Pan-African Communication Behaviors" or "African Language Systems."[10] The board members elaborated:

> .... African Language Systems are genetically based and not a dialect of English...[S]tudies demonstrate that such West and Niger-Congo African languages have been officially recognized, are worthy of study, understanding or application of its principles, laws and structures for the benefit of African-American students both in terms of positive appreciation of the language and these students' acquisition and mastery of English language skills.[11]

The resolution builds on legislation that had been passed by the California State Legislature recognizing the unique language stature of descendants of slaves that had been vetoed by various governors.[12] The Oakland Resolution also builds on the Federal Bilingual Education Act (20 U.S.C. 1402 et seq.) that mandated implementation of instructional programs for children of limited English proficiency. The Oakland School District receives $14 million in funding to accomplish this with additional sums provided by the Federal Government.[13] School district board members requested use of some of these financial resources. The funds were collected from public taxes paid in part by African American parents. Ebonics' use as a strategy to build English language proficiency had the goal of rectifying educational inequities that translate into economic inequities in employment.

The Ebonics topic surfaced in a formal way in 1969 when the American Speech Language-Hearing Association formed an office of Urban and Ethnic Affairs (today the Office of Multicultural Affairs) to focus on speech and language therapeutic needs of communities of color. In 1971, the Center for Applied Linguistics, based in Washington, D.C. developed a series of "dialect readers" called "Black English" as parts of a reading program.[14] Parents criticized the strategy heavily. Indications are that the readers did not use African language correlation. The "dialect readers" contained phonetic approximations of expressions and were difficult for children to use. The readers are not currently in print.[15] Scholars, nevertheless, continued their investigation of "Black English."

In 1973, Dr. Robert L. Williams and Ernie A. Smith conducted studies of cognitive and language development of Black children with funding from the National Institute of Mental Health. Dr. Williams is an emeritus professor of psychology and African American Studies at Washington University in St. Louis, Missouri. Smith is the Southern California linguist who coined the term "Ebonics."[16] Dr. Williams told a US Senate committee in 1996 that "... Ebonics is a valuable tool for teachers to use to prevent minority students from falling behind."[17] Though the seven members of the Oakland School Board voted January 15, 1997 to amend its December 18, 1996 Ebonics resolution deleting the term "genetically based," the Board concurred with Dr. Williams's view.[18] Board members have maintained that Ebonics does not have to be taught. Students come to school with their unique language formations that should be acknowledged and not viewed simply as substandard English.

Communities divide and debate the 'Ebonics' issue fearing that it is another trap to miseducate youth. At the core of the debate is the need to recognize and build on the reservoir of intellect, creativity and linguistic formations African American children bring to the classroom via their African heritage. Yet these language formations require careful unraveling.

Such expressions as 'I says,' or the double negative 'ain't no' (for example Marvin Gaye and Tammie Terrell 'Ain't no Mountain High Enough') can be heard in the British Isles. These expressions are sometimes considered archaic English rather than poor grammar. African American speech patterns can include such unique features as rhyme, rhythmic patterns, repetition, gestures, parables encoded in speech, alliteration and tone.[19]

The sources of other expressions – 'pacific' instead of 'specific,' 'baf' instead of 'bath,' 'mines' instead of 'mine,' 'womens,' or 'mens' instead of 'women' or 'men,' and 'skreet' instead of 'street' are more difficult to pin-point. Moreover, such verb forms as 'lernt' instead of 'learned' may be of German or Dutch origin.   It is important to remember that African American linguistic formations have been influenced by a multiplicity of European languages — English, French, Spanish, Portuguese, German,

Dutch, and even Danish from the Danish West Indies now the US Virgin Islands and St. Thomas.   Since the 1780s, the US has had a resident African American population with a Portuguese linguistic connection though it has been mixed with an African language base to form Cape Verdian Crioulo.[20] None of these observations preclude the fact that some English words are perhaps pronounced incorrectly and/or uniquely. This tendency can be found in com-

Fig. 2:   Kwame Nkrumah, first   munities across racial, ethnic and
President of modern Ghana.   regional lines.[21]

The Ebonics debate on language extends further. It is linked to African cultural heritage. Defenders of slav-ery denied that captives had one. Generations born in the US had never stepped foot in their ancestral home. But Africans transported in the 1600s through the 1800s knew of their families and traditions.

The 20th and 21st century debate on Ebonics raises questions about what remains of this African heritage. Langston Hughes, Melville Herkovits, W.E.B.DuBois and many others acknowledged the African cultural and lin-guistic connections to African Americans. Herskovits's critics could not deny his documentation of African religious and cultural survivals, but they pointed to the fact that his examples came predominantly from the

Caribbean/West Indies and South America rather than the US.[22] Moreoever, such scholars as Ralph J. Bunche and Abram Harris concluded that Africa did not remain "... an important aspect of the cultural identity of the Negro."[23]

Harvard University's Rupert Emerson added his observations as well. The relationship of the African Americans to Africa continues to be, ambiguous, hesitant and divided. He wrote:

> To a tragic extent the Negro has denied the African phase of his heritage by accepting the low opinion of Africa and Africans characteristic of the white-dominated society in which he lives...The African, it was asserted, had no history or distinctive culture of his own....[24]

Yet according to some accounts, African identity had not been obscured. For example, when Kwame Nkrumah, the first President of modern Ghana, arrived in Harlem, New York in the 1930s, he wrote "I felt immediately at home in Harlem and sometimes found it difficult to believe that this was not Accra."[25] Nkrumah supported the view "... that there were still African survivals in the United States and that the Negro of America" had in no way lost his cultural contact with the African continent.[26] These varied comments show the complexity of scholarly analysis of the African/African American connection. This general debate on retention of African linguistic patterns is perhaps the core of the Ebonics debate.

Despite the assault on African languages and cosmological traditions during slavery, it is worthwhile to explore points raised by the 'Ebonics' discussion. The OUSD coined the phrase, Pan African language system, without defining it.[27] The concept is, nevertheless, useful. 'Pan' refers to many and it is likely that captured Africans came from a number of linguistic regional backgrounds including the West Africa region. 'Pan' also identifies itself with the history of Pan-Africanism in the thrust to claim all of Africa rather than relegate the location to an 'ethnic' group.

The language debate might take into consideration the geographical configurations of Africa in the 1500s through 1800s when the slave trade occurred and boundaries differed from those of modern African countries.

Captured Africans, the ancestors of contemporary African Americans, came from areas where people and cultures defined polities, which were usually multiethnic and multilingual.[28]

The Mandinka (Mandingos) and Malinke lived in what is now Senegal, Guinea, Mali, the Ivory Coast and Burkina Faso (formerly Upper Volta). The Wolof lived in what is now Gambia and Senegal. The Mano communities are in northern Liberia (Ducoh) and southern Guinea. The Mende (Mendı) and Temne (Temni) lived between Liberia and Sierra Leone. The Fulani/Fulbe (called Peul in Senegambia) and Turkulor were spread among regions of present day Guinea, Cameroon, Nigeria, Liberia, Chad and Niger.[29]

Within the Voltaic family, the Senufos were between Ivory Coast, Burkina Faso and Mali. Within the Guinean family, the Ewe resided in Ghana and the Kotokoli and Chakossi kingdoms which form parts of modern Togo. (Guinea is a term of Portuguese origin to describe the coins made from gold taken from the region.) The Yoruba were in Nigeria, Togo and Benin. Bini is an uncomplimentary reference to Yoruba speakers in Benin. Meanwhile, Igbo, Efik, Ibibio and Ijo communities clustered into what is now eastern Nigeria. The Akan lived in Ghana and Ivory Coast. The Fanti, part of the Akan cluster, also resided in Ghana.[30]

Within the Saharan family, the Tubus were in Niger, Chad and Lybia. Within the Kushitic family, the Somali, Afars and Issas were distributed between the former Italian Somalia and the Afars and Issas (formerly Djibouti or French Somalia), lived in Kenya and Ethiopia.[31]

The Bakongo (Kongos), Balunda, Bakuba, Baluba lived in what is now Congo (Brazzaville), Angola, Gabon and former Zaire, now the Democratic Republic of Congo (Kinshasa). Ovambo Herero lived in what is now Angola and Namibia. Balundas lived in what is now Zambia. Xhosa, Ngonis, and Swazi resided between South Africa and Swaziland (Ngwane), while Matabele, Ndebele, and Shona communities encompassed contemporary Zimbabwe, Mozambique, and Zambia. The Sothos lived in Lesoto (formerly Basutoland), Botswana (formerly Bechuanaland) and South Africa. The Hausa emirates were spread among Northern Cameroon, Nigeria, and Niger.[32]

The Swahili resided in Tanzania (including Zanzibar), Somalia, Kenya, and Comoro Islands. Yao lived mainly in current day Tanzania and Gikuyu in Kenya; the Turkana between Kenya and Uganda. Migratory communities like the Maasai were split between Kenya and Tanzania. The Fang were in migration when 19th century colonial boundaries were set and became caught in political units of Gabon, Cameroon, and Equatorial Guinea that formed parts of the French and Spanish empires.

Similar multiethnic configurations could be found in the kingdoms of Buganda, Bunyuro-Kitara or Toro, modern Uganda and Rwanda and Urundi, now Burundi. Some African scholars note that the shifting of communities was easy due to the absence of borders which facilitated the formation of four cultural areas – the Sudanese, Guinean, southern equitorial, and eastern. Islam and Arabic also linked communities in various parts of the continent.

These remarks on Africa's changing geographical and linguistic clusters are by no means conclusive. This discussion is connected, however, to the Ebonics issue. While the OUSD resolution identifies Pan African communication patterns and the Niger-Congo Rivers' confluence as the source of some of African American speech, pinpointing the base of languages that Africans brought to the Americas requires knowledge of geopolitical configurations during the slave trade from the 1600s to 1800s. The point of origin of the ancestors of some African Americans can possibly be located by researching the records of such slave fortresses as Elmina (Ghana), Bunce Island (Sierra Leone) and Gorée (Senegal) and the 1998 W.E.B. DuBois Institute at Harvard University data base of some 27,233 voyages of slave ships from 1527 to 1867.[33] But given African residential patterns and the general disruption of some communities due to the slave trade, an identity complication occurs if one considers the plausibility that captured Africans may have begun their forced migration to the Americas by embarking from ports which were not their natal homes.

THE NUMBER OF AFRICAN LANGUAGES & CLASSIFICATION

The discussion can become quite entangled as to the number and location of various African languages. One observer writes: "As far as the number of languages is concerned, the situation is markedly worse than it is in relation to people, since a number of disputes still rage over identification and interrelationship of African languages and dialects."[34]

According to the observer, Africa has between one and two thousand languages. Of these languages, only a few such as Kiswahili (Swahili), Hausa, Amarigna (Amharic), Igbo, Yoruba and Somali are spoken by more than a million people. None of the languages embraces as many as twenty million, while very limited communities use the great bulk of "between one and two thousand."[35] Such comments, often projected as authoritative facts, might consider the invention of 'tribes' and paramouncies. For example, in East Africa on the north side of Lake Tanganyika, British imperialists formed the Nyakyusa "tribe" from the Kukuwe and Selya and two other communities.[36] South of Lake Nyanza where related but separate communities resided, the British gathered together the Usumbwa, Kwimba, Buzinza and others to form another new 'tribe' the Sukuma tribe. 'Sukuma' meant 'north' in the language of their Nyamwezi neighbors.[37] These examples indicate the care needed in numerical and regional assessments of Africa's linguistic traditions.

Other factors have also influenced the mis-numbering of African languages. For example, one reference classifies "Bamileke," as a language in Cameroon, although the term is generally applied to a historic economic community.[38] Moreover, clan groups have been counted by some linguists as separate 'tribes' with separate languages although, in some cases, these clans formed Africa's multiethnic polities sharing common ancestors and ancestresses.

Despite the varying and at times confusing perspectives on the number of African languages and their location, the discussion is connected to the Ebonics debate in that it is possible that individuals from parts of the continent besides West Africa slaved on plantations from the 1600s through 1800s. Archaeological sources indicate that Africans brought to the

Americas via the slave trade may have included individuals from the Indian Ocean African islands. Excavations of the African burial ground in New York, thought to hold up to 10,000 graves, have uncovered artifacts not only from West Africa, but from the Indian Ocean African kingdom of Madagascar as well. Moreover, records document that captured Africans from Mozambique who spoke MaShona and from Mali who spoke Senufo or possibly Arabic also became part of the American slave community.[39] Any analysis of African American speech and African culture would have to involve a wide continental geographical range.

The Ebonics discussion is deeply linked also to the ongoing research into the classification of African languages. Scholars have designed flow charts of the Niger-Congo Rivers region linking Kwa (a coastal area) and offshoot languages Akan, Gbe, Yoruba, Nupe, and Igbo with the Benue-Congo branch and its linguistic offshoots Ibibio and Bantu.[40]

Some linguists use such problematic terms as "Bantu" which has little meaning in the sense of identifying a specific language. Indeed "Bantu" might be derived from "Abantu," a Luganda expression which means "all these people."[41] Luganda is spoken in Buganda, Toro, Ankole and other areas of present-day Uganda.

Researchers explore other linguistic breakdowns. For example, Tshi-Luba (Congo) and Luba Kasai and Luba Katanga are attempts to classify the speech of Baluba communities based on the Tshi which is a river, the Kasai which a basin, and the Katanga mineral province of present day Congo Democratic Republic (Zaire). Scholars also challenge each other's spellings of terms. One writes Tshi-Luba and another writes Chiluba to refer to the same regional speech pattern.[42] These attempts at classification can become quite detailed as scholars search simultaneously for similarities and differences in African languages. Yet evidence suggests the linkage of languages previously thought to be separate and distinct noting that all African languages might derive from four clusters – Niger Congo, Nilo-Saharan, Afro-Asiatic or Kushitic-Ethiopic.[43] Preparers of the electronic encyclopedia, *Microsoft Encarta*, delineate four language clusters – Afro-Asiatic, Niger-

pa	pu	pe	peh	poh	po	bi	ba	bu	be
ba	bu	be	beh	boh	bo	mbi	mba	mbu	mbe
kpa	kpu	kpe	kpeh	kpoh	kpo			mgba	mgbi
gba	gbu	gbe	gbeh	gboh	gbo	fi	fa	fu	fe
va	vu	ve	veh	voh	vo	ti	ta	tu	te
da	du	de	deh	doh	do		la	lu	le
qa	qu	qe	qeh	qoh	qo	ndi	nda	ndu	nde
sa	su	se	seh	soh	so	zi	za	zu	ze
ca	cu	ce	ceh	coh	co		ja	ju	je
nja	nju	nje	njeh	njoh	njo	yi	ya	yu	ye

Fig. 3:   Example of Vai script.

Congo, Nilo-Saharan and Khoisan. African scholar Théophile Obenga asserts that these designations are imposed on African linguists by European and Euro-American educators. Obenga challenges the Afro-Asiatic category. His research finds etymological evidence connecting a number of African linguistic terms, grammar, and syntax to the various forms of the Ancient Egyptian language that lasted for 5,000 years. Obenga writes that Ancient Egyptian, Middle or Classical Egyptian, neo-Egyptian, Demotic Coptic, Ethiopic and Ge'ez originated in Africa, not Asia. Ancient Egyptian metaphysical notions, for example, the "ba," the soul, which is released at death, can be found in the whole of Black Africa. Use of the muffled dorso-velar occlusive /k/ and vowel sounds, and "ka" as a particle to form the distant future are used by the Hausa (Nigeria), Baguirmien (Chad), Fang (Gabon), Mbochi (Congo), Kimbundu (Angola) and Bambara (Mali).[43]

Moreover, John A. Umeh, writing on his Igbo heritage in Nigeria, traces his maternal grandparents' lineage to ancient Egypt. Senegalese scholar Chiek Anta Diop found similarities and, sometimes, identical vocabulary in his comparative research on Ancient Egyptian and the Wolof languages. Linguists who drafted a Hausa grammar text acknowledged that the language is most dominant in Northern Nigeria and spoken in large parts of West Africa, but it is "genetically related to such well-known languages as ancient hieroglyphic Egyptian, and also of importance [in] Amharic and Somali."[44]

Fig. 4   Olaudah Equiano was an Igbo from the eastern part of contemporary Nigeria.

Indeed similar terms, sometimes with similar and sometimes with different meanings appear in Hausa, Kiswahili, Amarigna (Amharic) and Fula.[45] The relevance of these issues to the Ebonics topic is again to signal the need to broaden the scope of inquiry into the origin of African American speech patterns.

In the public debate regarding "Ebonics," it might be pointed out that Africans had written languages, Akan Adinkra and pictographs.[46] Africans arrived on these shores with their own writing systems which included Vai and Wolof.[47] Muslim Africans were often literate in Arabic.[48] But slaveholders viewed African writing, the Akan Adinkra and other symbolic pictographs as evil and use of them was cause for a beating, sale or worse. Moreover symbols and African linguistic tones could not easily be transposed into Greco-Latin-Roman alphabetical script.[49]

Yet excavations in 1991 of New York City's African Burial site uncovered a plot containing the *Sankofa* Adinkra (which translates go back and fetch it, i.e., the past is not static but active, regenerative).[50] It is an Akan symbol attributed to an African sovereign from what is now Ivory Coast although the Adinkra symbols are most often associated with modern Ghana. But Akan speakers lived in parts of present-day Ivory Coast and Kotokoli or Togo in addition to Ghana. The ancestor who traced the 'Sankofa' Adinkra could have come from any of these places.

The use of African writing scripts by African Americans did not survive into the 1990's and the loss of these writing systems is a reminder of slavery's devastating erosion of language. Yet records exist of Africans who knew their linguistic lineage. One can glimpse aspects of African linguistic ties in the 18th and 19th accounts of the ancestors of 20th and 21st century African Americans.

Captured in Africa and enslaved in the Caribbean, colonial Virginia and England, Olaudah Equiano was an Igbo from the eastern part of contemporary of Nigeria. He was given the slave name Gustavus Vassa. "Traveling through Africa," Equiano noted that "...the languages of different nations did not totally differ, nor were they so copious as those of the Europeans, particularly the English. They were, therefore, easily learned and while I was journeying thus through Africa, I acquired two or three different tongues."[51] He used Igbo in his autobiography too. Equiano described the social structure of his area that included "*nze nzu*" local priests who were "Ah-affoe-way-cah/Ah-affoe," calculators of years "Ofo-nwanchi" and "afo-nwa-ika."[52] He explained that his name "Olaudah," signified vicissitude or fortunate and "Ola" or ring is a symbol of good fortune to the Igbo.[53] Interestingly, Ola is also an African American female personal name.

The linguistic heritage of other captured Africans has also been documented. In 1839, Sing-gbe (also Sengbeh Pieh or Cingue), a Mende (Mendi) speaker from Sierra Leone, led captured Africans in a revolt on the Cuban-Spanish slave schooner, *La Amistad*. Kaw-we-li, who had escaped slavery and joined the British Navy and whose English name was James Covey, was also from Mende country. He happened to be in New York and served as an interpreter for the African captives from the *La Amistad* who were tried and ultimately freed in Connecticut.[54]

One of the thirty-nine captured Africans included Kimbo who spoke Mende and explained the following counting system: "... 1, *etá*; 2, *fili*; 3, *kiau-wá*, 4, *náeni*; 5, *loélu*; 6, *wêta*; 7, *wafurá*; 8 *wayapá* 9, *tá-u*; 10, *pu*."[55] Gilabaru (Grab-eau) was born a Fulu in Mende country and was also among the surviving former captives. He explained that in his home, he had seen people write "... from right to left."[56] Besides Mende, he spoke Vai, Kon-no and Gissi.

A Yoruba connection took root too. Not only did captured Yoruba toil on US plantations, but some Yoruba were ex-militiamen from the British troops who fought in the American War of Independence. Many relocated and could be found in the 3rd and 5th Company villages in parts of Trinidad. Although 19th century African American Martin Delany cited a multiethnic heritage of Gola, Mandinka and Dey (in modern Liberia), he journeyed to Abeokuta among the Egba Yoruba.[57] Yoruba expressions endured however and are cited in chapters which follow.

The African language heritage, although known, was not always used by some Africans. Phillis Wheatley was from Senegambia, the home of Fula and Wolof linguistic communities. She wrote in eloquent English prose describing her experience of being ripped from her father's arms as a child and enslaved in Massachusetts.[58]

The African American slave community consisted of others who knew their ancestry. Enslaved in Connecticut, Broteer Furro also known as Venture Smith, was from Dukandarra in Guinea where Susu and Mano are spoken.[59]

The linguistic heritage is recorded in the account of Abd-ar Rahman Ibrahima. Ibrahima, known as Prince on the plantation, was indeed a West African prince from a wealthy Fulani (Fulbe) family. One source describes his home as the kingdom of Tambo in the Gambia (Senegambia), while another source lists his birthplace as the village of Timbo in what is now Equatorial Guinea. Accounts agree, however, that he was sold into slavery in New Orleans, Louisiana in 1788 at the age of 26 and ended up in Natchez, Mississippi. Ibrahima was a Muslim and he was multilingual which was not extraordinary for most continental Africans. He spoke Fula, Arabic, and possibly Wolof and Mende.[60]

In 1819 Charles Wilson Peale painted the portrait of African Yarrow Mamout, who lived in Georgetown and Maryland, and claimed to be more than a hundred years old. Peale recorded in his diary that Mamout was "noted for sobriety & a cheerful conduct... [He] professes to be a Mahometan, and is often seen and heard in the Streets singing praises to God."[61] The portrait of Mamout remains the most vivid documentation of his life.

Much more information is available about Suleiman Ibrahima Diallo or Job Ben Solomon, an eigthteenth century slave who eventually obtained his freedom. He came from a prominent Fulani family, was captured and sold to Captain Pike of the slave ship *Arabella* that landed in Annapolis, Maryland. After obtaining his freedom, Diallo returned to Africa and reached his village in 1735. He served as a liason preventing many of his people from being sold into slavery by paying ransoms for them to the British slave trading Royal African Company. Diallo wrote in Arabic. Diallo also wrote a memoir which Thomas Bluett edited and published entitled *Some Memoirs of the Life of Job, the son of Solomon, the High Priest of Boonda in Africa, Who was a Slave ...was set free... and sent to his native Land in the Year 1734*. The account is one of the first memoirs of a black person printed in English.[62] Omar ibn Sayyid,

who left at least fourteen Arabic manuscripts, was an Islamic scholar from Futa Toro (present day Senegal). Enslaved in North Carolina, he died in 1864, still a slave. History offers other examples as well. Mohammed Ben Sayyid, born near Lake Chad, was captured and enslaved in Europe then freed in 1860, came to the US, and fought in the War between the States (the Civil War) from 1861-1865. The *Atlantic Monthly* magazine published his autobiography in 1867. In the 1930s, the Works Progress

Fig. 5:   Frederick Douglass

Administration interviewed Georgia Sea Islanders who described Muslim rituals of their ancestors.[63]

Frederick Douglass, who taught himself to read and write, is known most for his eloquent writings in English. But his grandmother Betsey Bailey's patrilineage was from southern Nigeria.[64] Douglass has left an important commentary on the persistence of African language and its adaptation on the plantation where he was enslaved. He described the language spoken on the Lloyd plantation in Maryland.

> There is not, probably, in the whole south a plantation where the English language is more imperfectly spoken than on Col. Lloyd's. It is a mixture of Guinea and everything else you please. At the time of which I am now writing, there were slaves there who had been brought from the coast of Africa. They never used the "s" in indication of the possessive case. and me they called "Captain Athony Fed." Cap'n Ant'ney Tom," "Lloyd Bill," "Aunt Rose Harry," means "Captain Athony's Tom," "Lloyd's Bill," &c. "Oo you dem long to?" means, "Whom do you belong to?" "Oo dem got any peachy?" means "Have you got any peaches?" This language was spoken by all slaves on the Lloyd plantation - field hands and artisans.[65]

Douglass used an occasional African word too. He wrote, "My grandmother afforded relief from [a] journey of 12 miles by "toteing" me on her shoulder."[66]

Some researchers connect the word to a Latin base 'tollit.' But recent scholarship points strongly to its African origins: *tota* from Konga/Kikonga/Gullah meaning to pick up or to take; *tuta* from Kimbundu meaning to carry or a load; *tot* from Sierra Leone and *tut* from Cameroon.[67]

Other African Americans knew their heritage too. Pan Africanist Alexander Crummell's father was Temne from Sierra Leone. Regarding the continued usage of African languages, Professor Sterling Stuckey elaborated that African languages could still be heard in New York particularly in Albany where the Pinkster Festival of African drama, music, dance and historical pageantry was celebrated until it was quashed by officials in 1865. But this tradition made an appearance in American literature. James Fennimore Cooper's vivid description of Pinkster, a festival possibly of Dutch origin, appears in his novel about the town, *Satanstoe*, published in 1845. The scene was set in 1757 in New York City in the fields at the head of Broadway. The celebration began after Easter on Whitsunday or the Feast of the Pentecost when three days were devoted to the "great Saturnalis of New York blacks."[68]

Cooper wrote that nine-tenths of the blacks of the city, and of the whole country within thirty or forty miles collected in the thousands in those fields,

Fig. 6:   W.E.B. DuBois

beating drums, and singing African songs. Cooper emphasized that the features that distinguished Pinkster from the usual scenes at fairs, and other merry-makings were of African origin. It is true, Cooper explained, that there are not many blacks among the general populace of African birth; but the traditions and usages of their original country were so far preserved as to produce a marked difference between this festival and one of European origin. Some of these traditions involved making music, by beating on skins drawn over the ends of hollow logs, while other participants at Pinkster were dancing to the music. These hollow logs are in fact identical to the large drums played in African societies.

Several factors took a terrible toll on the active use of African languages. These included the sale of the mother – the primary transmitter of language, the disruption of family, and the deliberate destruction of language through seasoning, rape, torture, and psychological abuse.

The slave ships continued to arrive, however, despite the US Constitution's prohibition of the slave trade after 1808. Historians Duignan and Gann, for example, chart the arrival of slave ships: *Spitfire* in 1844; *Senator* and *Fame* in 1847; *Herald* in 1848; *Julia Moulton* in 1854; *P. Soule* in 1855; *W.D. Miller* and *Paez* in 1857; *Putnam and Haidee* in 1858; *Brutus, Bogota, Wildfire (Wildlife), Williams,* and an Unnamed slaver in 1860; and the *John Bell* in 1861. Between 1858 and 1861, the *Wanderer* and *Clothide* smuggled captured Africans into the Georgia

Sea Islands, the Mobile River of Alabama, South Carolina and the Florida Keys. Duignan and Gann list the US Navy's interception of the slaver, *Huntress* in 1864, as war raged in the United States.[69]

This record magnifies the tragedy of the slave trade. But it also indicates that well into the 19th century, Africans brought their own languages to US shores. The passage of time did disrupt active memory of precise African linguistic origin. Yet because of the continued arrival of African language speakers who interspersed among the African American community, it likely that African linguistic patterns persisted too.

DuBois, for example, provided a poignant account of the resilience of African language ties dating from the 1700s. Writing in the 1920s, DuBois began:

> My own people were part of a great clan. Fully two hundred years before, Tom Burghardt had come through the western pass from the Hudson with his Dutch captor, "Coenraet Burghardt," sullen in his slavery and achieving his freedom by volunteering for the Revolution (1776-1781/1783) at a time of sudden alarm. [70]

DuBois continued:

> His wife was a little, black Bantu woman who never became reconciled to this strange land; she clasped her knees and rocked and crooned:
> "Do bana coba--gene me, gene me!
> Ben d'nuli, ben d'le—"[71]

DuBois wrote: "With Africa I had only one direct cultural connection and that was the African melody which my great-grandmother used to sing."[72]

The late Supreme Court Justice Thurgood Marshall is not known to have spoken any African language. But he took pride in his African heritage and knew that his great-grandfather was from the Congo region. Marshall's paternal ancestor had been enslaved in the Eastern shore of Maryland.[73]

Comparatively and most interestingly, despite Bunche's view that the African connection had no impact on 20th century African Americans, Bunche showed his interest in African languages. In the 1930s, he took lessons in Kiswahili from Jomo Kenyatta, the future President of independent

Kenya. Bunche acknowledged his heritage too. When Bunche visited Kenya he told some of the Kenyans he met of his African ancestors who had been carried across the water and enslaved in a strange land, later freed and began to prosper. He expressed happiness to come back to his ancestral home. Bunche wrote that an elder welcomed him and gave him the name "Karioki" meaning "He who has returned from the dead."[74] Bunche described various aspects of the local society using the Gikuyu (Kikuyu) African terms: "mbari" meaning family group, "riika rimwe" meaning age-group "moherega" meaning clan, and "githakas (ithaka)" describing the system of hunting rights and land tenure.[75]

It should be noted, however, that Bunche did not agree that the rural black communities of the United States were more akin to rural African communities. He contrasted African communities in Togo and Dahomey, where he conducted field research, to "Negro life in this country."[76] He cited the lack of unity of the African population, many languages, "tribal" organization, and long-established customs and institutions of native life which place it in extreme contrast with Negro life of this country.[77] For Bunche and indeed for many contemporary African Americans, coming to terms with their African cultural and linguistic heritage, has not been an easy endeavor.

This chapter ends with several thoughts. The Ebonics issue has a long history. The discourse is entwined with the public policy on education and, in particular, bilingual instruction. Scholarly inquiry, moreover, requires careful analysis of African languages and the ways in which they have and have not merged with American English. Examples have been offered of Africans who arrived on these shores with a rich linguistic tradition. Such scholars as Anita De Franz offer salient thoughts for critics of Ebonics in "Coming to Cultural and Linguistic Awakening: An African and African American Educational Vision" in Jean Frederickson's edited volume on bilingual education.[78] Subsequent chapters of this study explore the issue further, probing expressions, names, vocabulary, and grammatical structures in African American speech to unravel what might not and what might remain of those ancestral African communication patterns.

CHAPTER II

AFRICAN LANGUAGES: TERMS, CREOLE, NAMES, GRAMMAR & VOCABULARY

A real impediment to the retention of some African language expressions is their uniqueness. English has no real parallels for some African language terms. These include genderless expressions, for example, in Igbo – "*numadu*," "*O*," or "*nya*."[1] Some terms found English translations. Perhaps reverence for the Igbo concept of *chi*, the Akan term *okra* or the Nile Valley hieroglyph *ba* meaning soul and the spirit force were transfered into the English expression of 'soul.' The word appears in a variety of contexts: soul food, soul talk, soul handshake, soul brother, soul sister, and soul mate.[2]

Other African cosmological concepts have appeared periodically in the 20th century, but for most African Americans the knowledge of their African religious heritage eludes them even though these concepts did survive among the Gullah and Geechee communities of the US. However, African American usage of the names of the Yoruba orisa or the Akan ultimate ancestor and creative 'Nan' have been overshadowed by usage of English and US religious traditions. 'Nan' has the day name Saturday. *Nana Nyankopon*

Kwaame or *Nyame* express the omnipotence of God, the creative force of the universe.[3]

It is, nevertheless, too simplistic to conclude that African Americans retained nothing of their multilingual heritage. In one of African American author Ishmael Reed's novels, his character prepares ointments for a client indicating "She must bathe in this and it will place the vaporous evil *Ka* hovering above her sleep under arrest and cause it to disperse."[4] The *ka* is the element or power that gives the spirit, the *ba*, its existence within form, time and matter. Interestingly too, Reed titles his novel *Mumbo Jumbo* and provides the following etymology for the expression: "Mumbo Jumbo - Mandingo (Mandinka) ma-ma-gyo-mbo, magician who makes the troubled spirts of ancestors go away: ma-ma, grandmother + gyo, trouble + mbo, to leave."[5]

GEECHEE, GUICHEE, GULLAH & CREOLE LANGUAGES

The presence of the Geechee or Guichee and Gullah communities provides the clearest case study of the persistence of multiple African languages within the twenty first century African American community. Researchers debate the origin of the term Gullah. Vass has suggested that it came from *ngola*, a royal title. The Portuguese mispronounced the term and applied it to the area now called Angola. Other suggestions are that the term Gullah comes from the Gola community from Liberia while the term Geechee may have originated from the Kisi (Kissi) also from Liberia.[6]

Researchers also dispute the supposedly 'Bantu' origins of words in Gullah/Geechee speech; a thesis which Vass and Holloway offer. Manfredi has countered that some of these names or words are Akan, for example, 'Abby' or Aba and he notes that the genders of these names for males and females are mismatched.[7]

African American linguist, Lorenzo Turner, identified African language precedents. Synchronic qualities of African language usage persisted over time in diphthongs, verb tenses, consonants and vowel sounds for tongue position, phoneme, diacritics, and syntactical patterns spoken in the sea island communities of North and South Carolina and Georgia.[8]

Turner's study does not identify Gola words among his detailed etymological list of African expressions or names. But he does provide names, words, terms, and cities used variously as personal names and place names from Wolof, Malinke, Mandinka, Igbo, Bambara, Fula, Yoruba, Hausa, Temne, Ibibio, Fon, (Dahomey/Benin Republic) Vai, Akan (Twi, Ewe and Fanti), Ga, and Kimbundu terms from Central and Southern Africa. In the 1930s, a student from Sierra Leone working with Turner identified the language of a five-line dirge preserved by the Georgia Gullah family of Amelia Dawley in a dialect of Mende spoken only in a certain part of southern Sierra Leone. 'Amelia's Song' was passed down to her daughter Mary Moran. In the 1990s, she sang the song to researchers. Meanwhile in the interior village of Senehum Ngola in Sierra Leone, one of the grandmothers of Benndu Jabati, had preserved a similar song. A village elder knew that their kinsmen had been captured and taken away during the slave trade and predicted that they would return. They would be recognized by their song. In the 1990s, Mary did return to her African relatives and the epic event was filmed in "The Language You Cry In."[9]

From his study, Turner found other synchronic qualities. The inter-dental fricative "th" does not exist in Gullah or in the West African languages. In pronouncing English words with this sound, he noted, Gullah and West African speakers substitute /d/ and /t/, respectively for the voiced and voiceless varieties of "th."[10]

The American Heritage Dictionary elaborated further. In South Carolina and Georgia low country, African Americans used the African term det meaning 'heavy,' for example 'det rain' as in 'heavy' rain and 'det' shower or 'heavy' shower. Some listeners to these speech patterns concluded that "det" was mispronounced 'that.' Loan words from the Geechee (Gullah) assimilated back vowels as in "fa" (fall) and "saut" (salt)[11] These patterns penetrated the speech of white Americans in southern states.

Manfredi criticizes Turner's work as educated guesses rather than observations though Turner spent considerable time among the Gullah and Guichee communities and studied African languages. None of Turner's challengers have been able to provide evidence refuting the premise that African American speech, especially Gullah/Geechee (Guichee), contains elements of African languages. Some personal names, especially in the Gullah and Geechee communities in the African American community, are drawn from places. Examples are Kano from Northern Nigeria and Abomey from Dahomey (present day Benin).[12]

One of the most majestic portrayals of the Gullah/Guichee communities is Julie Dash's film "Daughters of the Dust" produced by Geechee Girls Productions.[13] Dash is a descendant of these African American Georgia Sea Islanders of the Peazant (Prizant) family. Filled with references to Africa, the film's setting unfolds on Igbo (Ibo) Landing. The family elder, Nana, recalls the sale of her enslaved mother. Nana is the generational link between the members of the family who were born in slavery and those who were born free. She says she is like the African Griot who remembered the family histories of birth and death. Among the members of the community of Igbo (Ibo) Landing is Bilal Mohammed, the African who crossed over the water (Atlantic Ocean) on the slave ship, the *Wanderer*.

In one of the scenes, Violet, one of the family members, calls the names of African deities, Obatala and Shango. Among the Gullah and Guichee, their Pan-African linguistic heritage maintained both a static or synchronic quality by continuing to use certain place and

Fig. 7 Yoruba orisha deity, Shango.

Fig. 8   Julie Dash, director, "Daughters of the Dust."

personal names.

The Gullah/Geechee and Cape Verdean Crioulo speakers have created Creole languages.[14] They merit preservation and comparative study to *Papiamento* spoken in the Dutch Antilles, Haitian Creole, or Trinidad's Creole based on the linguistic heritage from Yoruba and Hausa ancestors portrayed in Maureen Warner-Lewis's *Guinea's Other Suns.*[15]

NAMES

Names are deeply symbolic in African linguistic communication. Persons often receive multiple names commemorating rites of passage and significant transitions in life. According to Akan traditions, persons received an Akan natal day name and a name of an honorific titular god. Corresponding to each person's natal day name is his or her attribute or secret name.[16]

Examples of day names are: for males – Kwasi "He of Sunday"; Kwadwo (Kojo or Cudjoe) for Monday; Kwabena for Tuesday; Kwaku or Kweku for Wednesday; Yaw (Yao) for Thursday; Kofi for Friday; Kwame (Kwamena or Kwamina) for Saturday; and for females – Akosua, Asi, Esi or Essie (Sunday); Adwoa for Monday; Abena or Abenaa for Tuesday; Akua or Ekua for Wednesday; Yaa for Thursday; Afua or Efua for Friday; and Ama or Amma for Saturday. Other versions of these day names, usually for girls, are: Kwasida (Sunday); Dwowda (Monday); Benada (Tuesday); Wukuda or Wukuada (Wednesday); Yaoda or Yawoada (Thursday); Frida or Efiada (Friday); and Memenda (Saturday).[17]

In the 1700s and 1800s, records provide considerable evidence that Africans used their African language names. The spellings of the names var-

ied. Male personal names were adapted from their Akan language bases.
They included: Sunday – Quashee, Quashy, Quash, Quashy, Quashee instead
of Kwasi; Monday – Cudjo instead of Kwadwo; Tuesday – Cubbenah instead
of Kwabena or in Fanti, Kwamina; Wednesday – Quarcoe, Quaco or Kwaco
for Kwaku; Thursday – Quao for Yaw; Friday – Coffie, Cuffee, Cuffy instead
of Kofi; and Saturday – Quame for Kwame (Kwami). Quaw was used frequently as a male personal name and was a version of Kwasi, Kwadwo,
Kwabena, Kwaku or Kwame. Female personal day names also appeared with
some frequency: Sunday – Quasheba; Monday – Juba; Tuesday – Beneba;
Wednesday – Cuba; Thursday – Abba; Friday – Pheba, Phibbi; and Saturday
– Mimba.[18]

Blassingame and Berry estimate that between 5 and 10 percent of the given
names of free blacks were African derivatives: Quashy Baham, Wilson
Africa, Edward Affricaine, Kedar Africa, Elikaim Bardor, Byer Affrica,
Gadock Coffe, Pryor Biba, Alford Bim, Cuff Cawon and Ally Africa. Ally or
'Ali' means the 'Exalted' or 'The Most High' in Arabic.[19] Paul Cuffe, the
famed navigator and emigrationist of African and Wampanoag Native
American parentage, changed his surname of Slocum to honor his African
born father Kofi, which was spelled "Cuffe."[20]

This review of naming practices reveals additional examples of African linguistic ties. For example, Juba, one of the day names given to a male child
along the Guinea coast was also a nickname given to a girl born on Monday
in slave communities or used to describe a 'tomboy' (1620s-1800).[21] The
name Juba, which was fairly common among African men in the 17th and
18th centuries, is also the name of a region in modern Kenya/Somalia and
Sudan.[22]

Scholars point to the complexity of deriving the meaning of African names
or terms. African language lexical tones and pitch convey varied meanings
although the spelling may be same. For example "Sambo" is a Hausa name
given to the second son in the family. But in Mende and Vai, with a different pronunciation and intonation, "Sambo" can mean disgrace or misfor-

tune.[23]

The erosion of the usage of African names occurred too. Samba, meaning comfort in Wolof is still recalled in musical form in Brazil where there remains a strong African presence. A possible derivation of Samba is Zambo (from Southern/Central Africa) and it also means to give comfort. Other derivatives are Sambu in Mandinka and Sambo in Hausa.[24] The fact that the name was at one time fairly common and no longer used may be due to a song popularized by white Americans during the war from 1861-1865 "Sambo's Right To Be Kilt" and especially the derogatory usage of the name enshrined in the book *Little Black Sambo*.[25]

Fig. 9   The sambo figure, long ridiculed, is a Hausa name; also Sambono in Zambia.

Further damage occurred. Sambo, according to Dillard, has been used to represent a kind of pejorative of Samuel --Sam, Sammy, Sambo representing a kind of descending order of respect for the person being named. Stanley M. Elkins's, *Slavery, A Problem In American Institutional and Intellectual Life*, treated the name Sambo as the stereotype for a "docile, compliant"African American man.[26]

"Semantic pejoration" occurred with other names as well. Quasheba came to mean "the colored mistress of a white man" or even "a prostitute" while Quao came to mean "an ugly stupid man," and "Cuffie" a "contemptuous name for a Negro."[27] No doubt, these negative connotations discouraged usage of African names or if they were used, African Americans avoided overt recognition of the names' African origin. Such scholars as Blassingame and Berry commented that African appellations disappeared from the lists of slaves' names.[28]

Other names remained in the African American community and have strong affinity to African derivations. They are 'Gaye,' as in Marvin Gaye, possibly from 'Gueye' in Wolof communities of Senegal and Gambia; Esi (Essie) from Ewe and Fanti for a girl child born on Sunday and Bissi or 'Bessie' for the first- born girl of a family (possibly from Ewe).

Almost every African American family has someone called "Nana." "Nana" among the Akan community is connected with the "God concept Nyame" or "Nyankapon."[29] The concept conveys the connections among all kinds of families or community groups. According to Danquah, "Nana" or "Nyame" links the agnatic family of male ancestor and descendants; the cognatic family with the mother's brother, the uncle, as head, traced through the mother and the maternal grandmother; the clan or enlarged family; the larger admixture of cognates and agnates and clans, possessing one speech or dialect and common customs; and finally the state or nation-group with one family upraised or acknowledged by their moral or physical efficiency above the rest. The "Nana" is chosen from among them and accorded honor and held to be the exemplar of the Great Ancestor's creative source.[30] In modern Ghana, however, "Nana" (a genderless name) has evolved as a title in Akan, Nanny in Ewe and Nii in Ga. They are all equivalent to prince or princess.

African Americans may have lost the understanding of the deeper meaning of the term. Almost every African American family, however, has someone called "Nana." Ralph Bunche, for example, called his maternal grandmother who raised him, "Nana."[31] Nana can also be a part of a man's name to denote his matriclan and matrilineal descent as well.

It is, nevertheless, possible to hear expressions of African origin encoded in twenty first century English spoken by African Americans outside the Sea Islands. Lorenzo Turner pointed to expressions of African origin that some observers misinterpreted as mispronounced English. These included the Mende word *suwangc* meaning "to be proud of" which was viewed as a corruption of the English "to swagger"; the Wolof word "*lir*" meaning small, but viewed as a corruption of "little"; or the Twi word *fa* meaning "to take" has been explained as a mispronunciation of the word "for."[32]

Some sounds and expressions did not re-pronounce entirely and surface in altered form. For example, "a-go-go" is thought to be derived from *Ngongo* meaning assembly or meeting. It is the term for the traditional Council of Doula (Cameroon). Remember Smokey Robinson and the Miracles' "Going to a-go-go"?[33]

African terms are recalled in songs 'way down yonder in the paw-paw patch.' Paw-paw is still heard in parts of West Africa to refer to papaya.[34] Continued systematic etymological study is required to authenticate root words. But the following passages provide a small sampling of African words that fused with English spoken by African Americans.

The Fula language offers the following. The word *Jam*, meaning "peace, well being" appears in such expressions as *Jam tan* meaning "fine" or *Ñallen jam* meaning, "Good, Let's spend the day in peace."[35] In African American speech, 'jam' can mean 'a good party' or 'an enjoyable gathering or a difficult situation.' In Trinidadian speech it has the same contextual meaning.

Certain sounds and words came from Yoruba, but have usually been considered mispronounced English. For example, *fo* or to jump and *fa* to draw, stretch, to be slow, crawl, or glide.[36] It is quite possible that these words were intentionally used in the spiritual 'Swing low sweet chariot. Coming fo (fa) to carry me home.' 'To carry' appears twice: once in Yoruba and and once in English. The repetition serves as emphasis. Reduplication is a common feature of African languages.

Other words from Yoruba include *jiga* meaning jigger; *da* which means 'where is,' and possibly *bèè*, which means 'like that'; *bè* to exist, and *bé* to beg.[37] African American speech blurred the distinction between phrases such as: *bèè* 'like that,' *bè* to exist, and *bé* to beg. It is possible that expressions which are considered incorrect English grammar, 'I be like,' have African precedents on two levels. The Yoruba *bèè* has fused with the English /be/ and the repetition parallels a device used in many African languages to convey emphasis. Some examples are *Jù-Jú*, a Nigerian musical form.[38] Two major themes in *Jù-Jú* music have been the urban experience and the *ijin-lée* Yoruba tradition. But the term *Jù-jú* took on a negative connotation in English.[39]

Reduplication is also used, however, in the Geechee expression "done done" to emphasize "finished" or completed.

From Tshi-luba (Chiluba) in the Congo region come such words as 'Jambalaya' from *tshimboebole* meaning 'cooked corn' although the term is used in the US to describe a rice, vegetable and seafood dish. Jazz is said to be a derivative of the word *jaja* pronounced 'jas' or 'jass.' *Kingombo* meaning soup and is also a thick soup of okra and shrimp spiced with filé.   It is called 'gumbo' and it is eaten especially by African American communities in Louisiana and the Georgia Sea Islands. 'Jiggaboo' or 'jigabo' is from *tshikabo* meaning meek or servile and came to have very derisive meaning in English.[40]

From Ewondo, spoken in Cameroon, comes the word *nyam*. *Nyam* is used among the Serer in Senegal and is called *nyama* in Fula which is spoken throughout West and parts of Central Africa. It is *djambi* in Vai, *nyambi* in Southern Africa, and *njam* in Gullah. It has been used as 'yam' in English and erroneously applied to the sweet potato. *Nyam* has also been used as a verb meaning 'to eat.'[41] All over the English-speaking Caribbean *nyam* has precisely the same meaning as the African example.

In African American speech, there is the word 'jitterbug.' It is linked to *jito-bag* from Mandinka (1650s-1940s), and describes a dance-crazed person. In the 1940s, the jitterbug was the name of popular dance performed to swing jazz music.[42]

From possible Temne origin is the expression *yo* from Sierra Leone. It is an ending participle of an emphatic statement. It appears frequently in African American speech and adopted by some youth in other ethnic groups as well. Though the speakers may be unaware that the term is of African origin, "yo" persists in such expressions as in "Give me back my ball, Yo!"[43] The expression *ya* is used also as an emphatic ending participle. In Akan the same expression (*yo*) is used as consent in two or more exchanges and is often used at the end of someone's speech, sentence, or phrase. Some examples are: 'May God bless you!' '*Yo!*' or 'Have a good night my friend.' '*Yo!*'

Wolof offers examples of words or expressions that also appear in contemporary African American speech. *Jama* is a Wolof word meaning crowd or gathering. 'Jam' in African American speech can mean 'to fight or put someone in an awkward situation, to party or play music. Its uses range from the song title "Bad Mama Jama" to 'jam,' 'jamming,' and 'jamboree'.[44] These words have become a part of the national and international lexicon.

Other Wolof grammar constructions also have similarity to those in African American speech. For example *def* is the Wolof verb "to do" or "to make."[45] In Wolof, *djam* (Jam) means 'peace.' In African American parlance "def" is an adjective or adverb describing something of "excellent [or] highest praise."[46]

"Def jam" means literally "to make peace" and may have made its way into African American speech in the 1990s in "Def Comedy Jam."[47] The young African American producers who gave this name to their show may not be aware that these words are similar to words from their African language heritage.

The use of "Da" in African American speech also has an African precedent. *Da* (or *Dafa*) in Wolof meaning 'it' is an explicative predicator. For example: "*Da nga mun (-a) naan lool*." "It is that you drink too much" or "You drink too much."[48] Turner points out that *da* and *de*, appear frequently in African language constructions.[49]

Some African languages did not have a /th/ sound and Africans transferred the familiar sound *da* or *de* to use as a substitute.[50] But 'Da' is still used in contemporary speech as 'it' or 'it is' for example 'Da cold' or 'It is cold'.

Wolof also includes *Bii* and *Bee*. These terms were confused with the English verb root 'to be'. In Wolof, *Bii* and *Bee* function as 'you', a noun determiner to express distance.[51]

Some Wolof words have become so encoded in African American speech, but are often viewed as slang in English. For example, *hepi* meaning 'to see' and *hipi* meaning 'to open one's eyes' have become the common expressions 'I'm hip' or 'I'm hep' and are used by speakers outside the African American community.[52] Wolof has contributed the word *jev* to African American speech which is written 'jive' or 'jiving.' *Jev* is the verb 'to cry' although one source defines 'jive' or *jev* as false or careless talk.[53]

Words which have multiple African etymologies include "juke" or "jook" from *juka* in the Niger-Congo cluster; *dzug* from Wolof and in Gullah, for juke-house or jook house describing a roadside inn, type of music or loose life-style. "Juke" is also the root word of jukebox.[54] In Trinidadian slang "jook" is to stab, to poke, to cut and has sexual connotaions as in the African American example.

"May" is also a name used with some frequency and is possibly related to the Wolof verb *may* meaning 'to make a present of' and functions as a double object transitive verb.[55] The sound of 'may' differs from the Wolof *may* which is pronounced as two syllables instead of one. But the Wolof '*May*' and the English 'May' for the month overlapped in such personal names as Annie May, Eula May, Ula May, Beulah May or Mae.

Boo appears in Wolof as the temporal relative pronoun second person 'you'. For example: *Boo liggéé bee* meaning "When/if you (singular) work."[56] African Americans use 'Boo' as a nickname for a boy or girl.

In Wolof, *ma* is an object pronoun and the subject pronoun "I."[57] African American speech uses both the Wolof *ma* and the English 'my' to show possession.

Twi has also contributed words that have become part of African American speech: *kakate* meaning unmanageable or surly is used in English with the same definition and spelled "cockaty."[58] Another example is "jam," *dzaem* or *gyan*. When the Akan say that they are going to *dzaem* someone who is bereaved, they go in their numbers and sit around him or her. The English word /jam/ means "to crowd with people, cars" or other objects so that movement is difficult. Ghanaian scholar Osei writes that the Akan and English words are certainly cognates. It is interesting to note that virtually no phonological difference can be found between the two words.[59]

Other Twi words include *aboa* written 'boa' in English. The English word 'boa' refers to 'a big snake' while the Akan word *aboa* refers to any animal.

Osei writes that the two words are cognates. Indeed the only difference may be the stress with which the English word is pronounced.[60]

Mmoa in Akan is the plural of *aboa* and may be defined as 'animals.' Moa in English refers to a group of large birds that cannot fly. The Akan word *aseky_w* (*asIt__w*) refers to anything which has been twisted out of shape or out of the proper position. It appears in English as "askew" meaning "awry."[61] Osei suggests that the English and Akan words are cognates. A comparison of the two words reveals that the /I/ represented by letter /e/ that comes after /s/ is lost in the English version according to Osei.[62]

The tendency in African American speech to mute certain consonant sounds may have connections to other Akan words. For example, some African Americans pronounce 'barn' as 'ban.' The Akan word for this building used to store grain is *ban*. What appears to be mispronounced English is the correct pronunciation for the word in Twi.[63] A wall is also called *ban* in Akan. The English and Akan words are cognates. The only difference is the lengthening of the vowel /a/ reflected in the /r/ following the /a/ in the spelling of the English version.

Similarly, some African Americans leave off the 't' in some words. Sit is sometimes pronounced 'si'. Here again the Twi word *si* may explain the persistence of the pronunciation rather than incorrect English articulation. The Akan word *si* means 'to sit.' *Si* is also a verb that describes the setting down of anything that is stiff enough to hold itself upright. *Si* is used in the following translations. "The king is sitting in the palanguin" – *ohen no si apakan no mu* and 'Sit the child down on the bed', *Fa akwadaa no si mpa no so*. *Si* is also used in the translation of "the bucket is standing on the verander"– *bokiti no si abranaa no so*; and "the bottle is standing on the box" – *toa no si adaka no so*. The two words *si* and 'sit' are cognates. The Akan version is the proto form. *Si* is an open syllable while 'sit' is a closed syllable. The vowel in the Akan version is advanced while the vowel in the English version is "unadvanced."[64] Osei suggests that this African cognate came into the English language before the era of the slave trade. The connection to Ebonics, however, is that African Americans readily use words from their African experience when possible and particular pronunciations are not always incorrectly spoken English words although this does occur.

Additional examples of African vocabulary in African American speech have been uncovered. From southeastern Nigeria, the Igbo and Efik expression *mbakara* means "he who surrounds or governs," while *buckra* in Igbo means an European. In African American speech, particularly in the 18th and 19th centuries, the word was used to describe Europeans in general and had several etymologies: *backra, buckra, bakru, bokru, baccero, bochara, backra* and *buckra*. It also appears as *Buckroe*, pronounced *buckra*, and it is the name of a street in Hampton, Virginia.[65]

From Luganda comes the name of a character in a familiar children's film, *Bambi*, a term of endearment. The compiler of a volume on the origin of English words identifies such words as caterpillar as having African connections too. Joseph T. Shipley writes: "caterpillar is the hairy cat, see pilo [cattus] feminine, *catta*) may be of African origin."[66]

Researchers have suggested that other words of African origin survived. These words include *Mojo*. It refers to a charm and it is suggested that it comes from *muoyo* which means 'life.' It also describes a red flannel conjure bag from African-American hoodoo. African American blues singer Muddy Waters, McKinley Morganfield, sang "I got my mojo workin' but it just don't work on you." Jim Morrison, of the Doors rock group, used the term too in his "Mojo rising."[67]

Winifred Kellersberger Vass has suggested African derivations for such words as *moola* which refers to money or tax money and comes from *mulam-bo*; mosey from *muon-ji* meaning to work slowly or meandering; hulla-balloo from *halua balualua*; and gooly from *ngula*. Remember the Stylistics "Betcha By Gooly?"[68] Manfredi calls Vass's etymology absurd, but he corroborates the existence of African words noting many are 'Mandekan,' i.e., Mandinka, and Akan. He has no explanation, however, for words proven not to be of English origin. Vass's vocabulary list suggests other words from African language bases: "yackety-yack," derived from *yakula-yakula* – yack meaning a stupid person and also stupid conversation.[69]

PLACE NAMES

Vass has suggested place names originating possibly from "Bantu" or more precisely from African origins.   Vass admits that a certain Creolization occurred in language because of the mixture of Creek, Cherokee and Choctaw Native Americans and African communities in the southern US areas.   Indeed the word *siminoli*, anglicized as Seminole, is a Creek word meaning 'runaway' and used to describe the Creek who left Georgia and went to Florida.   African Americans who fled the plantations and joined Native American communities were also called *siminoli* or Black Seminoles.[70]

But other evidence suggests African origins of some place names.   Some of those names appear on road maps in the 1970s and 1990s.   They include the following examples from North Carolina: Ulah from *ula* meaning to purchase or buy; Aquone from *akuone* meaning let him scrape, scrub or shave off, referring to a sawmill or carpentry work.   The list includes Ela from *ela* meaning cast, throw, pitch, pour or pour out; Nakina from *nuakina* meaning hate, be cruel to or be mean to (plural imperative).   It is used in the expression, *Ngakina*, which conveys "I am hating, being cruel to.[71]

Virginia, Georgia and Missouri all have towns named Chula possibly derived from *Tchula* meaning frog or Chula from *Choctaw* meaning fox.   In South Carolina, there is a town called Alcolu possibly from the root word *alakana* meaning hope for, long for or to desire exceedingly, for example, freedom.   The town Ashepoo may be derived from *ashipe* meaning "let him kill." Manfredi suggested that Vass used an inacurrate transcription.   She wrote *ashipe* instead of *asipa* deleting the accent and adding an /h/.   It is important to note, however, that these accents are imposed on the language in attempts to transcribe African sounds into English.   It might be difficult to say which is more correct.   In any case the spellings of place names were recorded not by African Americans using their own African scripts but by white officials who tried to reproduce the sounds as best they could.[72]

In Mississippi, Vass has identified such town names as "Lula" from *lula* meaning be bitter, refuse to obey and "Osyka" from *oshika* meaning "burn up, catch on fire."[73] In Georgia, there are possibly such African derived place names as "Cataula" from *Katuulua* meaning 'he never comes' referring to an absentee master; "Suwanee" is from *Nsub'wanyi* meaning 'my house' or 'my home.' Georgia has such place names as "Cataula"; "Inaha" from *inaha* which means 'right here' or 'at this very place' and 'Zetella' from *Jetela* which means 'to be languid.'[74] Tennessee also has a town called Sewanee possibly derived from *Nsub'wanyi*.

In Florida, possible African place names include "Wauchula" from *Waujula*. In Alabama are such town names as 'Eufaula' from *Ubaula* meaning 'loot or pillage'; 'Chunchula' from the Luba expression *Tshutshuluka* meaning 'to be held back' or 'restrained;' 'Wedowee' from *Wetu wee* meaning 'our very own,' and 'Coatopa' from *Kuatupa* meaning 'to give them to us' referring to rations or supplies.[75] Delaware and Louisiana have towns named 'Angola' from *Ngola* which is actually the title of political officials in the Luanda kingdoms that the Portuguese called Angola.[76]

Manfredi criticizes Vass's approach and suggests she is ignorant of African languages though she too lived among communities of Central Africa. Some of Vass's work parallels that of African American missionary Althea Brown Edminston 's 1932 dictionary of "Bantu" words compiled while she worked in what was the Belgian Congo.[77] While conceding that Angola is of African origin and possibly *Chumukla* is derived from the *Tsiluba* (Chiluba), Manfredi provides no alternatives as to how other non-English place names, personal names, and words have come into the language patterns of African Americans nor does he provide the origins of place names which Vass maintained are not derived from the Creek, Choctaw or other communities.[78]

In addition to investigating place names, Vass wrote down songs. Although the exact African origin of the songs may be debated, it is unlikely that they came from the Creek and Choctaw, Cherokee or other original communities in what became the southern United States.[79]

While the origins of place names are intriguing, some African derivations seem to have survived in the 21st century. For example, Celey is the name of a street in Hampton, Virginia. Another street is "Quash." The latter is probably derived from *Kwasi* as is "Quassy Amusement Park" in Connecticut.[80]

AFRICAN GRAMMATICAL CONSTRUCTIONS

African languages had constructions that did not really transfer in meaning into African American speech. For example *na* which is sometimes considered a slurred pronunciation of 'no' was, nevertheless, a familiar sound. It persists in contemporary African American speech. *Na* in Wolof is a dependent subject predicator.[81]

Some African grammatical structures became widely used in English. A few examples offered by Osei include: >not= from the >n= The Ancient Egyptian negative indicator was the word >n= the hieroglyphic sign of which was n. This >n= has been maintained by the Akan till today.[81] This >n= sound is also used in African American speech.

Dem is a verb in Wolof meaning 'to leave.' It is used in the example, *Mangi dem na kër* meaning literally "I am leaving [to go] home" or "I am going home."[83] One source defines "dem" as a deliberate corruption of 'them,' but it may be the natural transfer of a familar sound although African American speech does not use 'dem' as the Wolof verb.

Some language terms were, nevertheless, lost. African American speech does not use Hausa expressions of possession *A na* plus >*da*=phrase. The perfective appears in such expressions as *Na Manta an fita da dabbobi*. The Hausa interrogative *ya* meaning >how= in English does not seem to be used either.[84]

FOLKLORE

Many cultures have folklore of written and oral traditions. African American tales use English as a communication medium, but the tales fuse African concepts and unique combinations of words of African and English origins.[85] Friday is ominous in African American folklore, so the saying goes. *Dayclean* is a Gullah word meaning "dawn" or "just before."[86] The late part of the day is known as *dayclean* from the expression "the sun is leaning toward the West."[87] "Every 'fore dayclean, Mom Bett was there to see first light fall over the tree."[88] "Then the gentlest 'fore-dawn came in, first in the corners, then shining on the flowers."[89]

Some folklore stories use African words in the title. For example, Jamal Koram the Story Man uses "the *Ashiko* drum," a type of Yoruba drum, in his tale "The Lion And The Ashiko Drum, A Fable From South Carolina."[90] Frankie and Doug Quimby told Marian E. Barnes "The Ibo [Igbo] Landing Story." It is the tragic story of Africans, Igbo, from what is now Nigeria, who were tricked into boarding a ship to St. Simon's Island on the east coast of Georgia. When they found out they were going to be sold as slaves, they drowned themselves in Dunbar Creek.[91]

African American folklore also encodes African proverbs, lessons of history and mythology. Some tales employ African parallels, language patterns and methods of storytelling. Various scholars maintain that African captives brought these traditions to the Americas. Berry and Blassingame point out that in 1966, Hugh Anthony Johnson, after studying more than 1,000 traditional Hausa and Fulani folktales in Nigeria, asserted that Brer Rabbit is undoubtedly the direct descendant of the hare of African folktales. Not only are his characteristics exactly the same as those of the Hausa *Zomo*, but the plots in at least thirteen of the Uncle Remus stories are parallels of those Hausa stories.[92]

Some of these tales are attributed to such white American writers as William J. Faulkner. But scholars point out that Simon Brown, a former slave from Virginia, told Faulkner such tales as "Brer Tiger and the Big Wind."[93]

For many years he worked for Faulkner's mother on the family farm in Mississippi. Brown told the stories to Faulkner who retold the tales in his writings.[94]

The use of personification in animal tales is also frequent in the writing of African American folklore. The Akan name for spider is Anansi and the little insect has a number of tales in which wit or other human character traits are portrayed.   African American folklore includes some spider tales although African American tales seem to use the Akan term Anansi less frequently than Caribbean writers of African descent.   For example, Louise Bennett has written a short story "Anancy An Him Story, A Tale From Jamaica." Marian E. Barnes has adapted and retold the spider tale in

"Anansi's Riding Horse, A Jamaican Folktale."[95] These tales and the format of African folklore represent a connection to an African linguistic heritage.

Chapter Two has continued the discourse on Ebonics by linking the discussion to synchronic qualities of African language usage that have persisted over time in diphthongs, verb tenses, consonants and vowel sounds for tongue position, phoneme, diacritics, and syntactical patterns. They are noticeable in various ways in African American communities, but especially in the sea island communities of North and South Carolina and Georgia. The following chapter looks at the contemporaneity of these linguistic patterns in Rap.

Fig. 10   Louise Bennett, folklorist/storyteller, pioneer in Jamaican nation-language.

Chapter III

Rap, Hip Hop, Games
Other Africanisms & Ebonics

The perversity and adverse influence on youth is often highlighted in public discourse on Rap music and Hip Hop culture. Although this criticism should not be dismissed, Rap, in its essence, is a part of African expressive orature. The performances of some Rap musicians, their songs, and storytelling are extensions and transformations of an ancient oral tradition. The penchant for profane behaviors, which some performers exhibit, should not be confused with African expressive culture. This chapter on Rap and Hip Hop culture begins with an exploration of their African links. The chapter unveils some of the current issues in Rap and Hip Hop orature; analyzes the song texts, delivery, and style of female and male artists. The chapter also presents song games and other examples of African and

African diasporan communication patterns.   Richard Majors and Janet Mancini Billson emphasize that West African culture has had "colossal impact on African-American culture."[1]   The two authors support their thesis using the analysis of W. Boykins.   He delineates several qualities of West African culture.   Some of the West African qualities are spirtualism, spontaneity, expressiveness, and a preference for oral and aural modes of communication.   Boykins contrasts these traits to the Euro-American cultural counterparts.   He states that the Euro-American mechanistic metaphor stresses materialism and mastery over nature while the African organic metaphor emphasizes expressive movement.[2]

WHAT IS AFRICAN ABOUT RAP & HIP HOP?

Oral virtuosity and the ability to use alliterative, metaphorically colorful and graphic forms of spoken language are central to African and African American rap-talking.   Clarence Major suggests in *Juba To Jive* that the term "Rap" has Sierra Leone origins and traces the use of the term "rap" in colonial America from the 1730s.[3]

Critics will challenge the idea that Rap and Hip Hop have African origins noting that African languages and instruments do not figure prominently in performances.   Occasional words of African origin such as *jam*, *jigga*, *jiggabo*, or *nana* do appear in some of the song performances.   African stringed instruments, for example, the kora (xora), xalam, and various drums like the bata, may not always be used in African American performances.   But African American musicians are rediscovering and using the traditional horn instruments from Mali, the kalimba thumb piano from the East Africa, Republic of Congo (formerly Zaire), and Zimbabwe or such drums as the asheka (ashiko), donno, Congo, and tabala.   Also aspects of African verbal patterns have survived with the adaptation of English into "black talk" with its special rhythms, inflections, songs, and grammar.[4]

Rap incorporates the rhyming technique, but moves beyond using rhyme

Fig. 11   Slick Rick (Ricky Walters)

only as a mnemonic aid. Rap becomes a test of ritualistic story-telling, verbal sparing, and improvisation which Rap musicians call free style. East-coast performers in particular emphasize semantics, using the voice to convey sarcasm, braggadocio, and demonstrative force. Slick Rick's (Ricky Walters) Rap "Street Talkin" from his 1999 release, *The Art of Storytelling*, provides an example of this lyrical virtuosity.

Author Marcyliena Morgan expounds on Rap and Hip Hop in her paper "Ain't nothin'but a G thang': Grammar, Variation and Language Ideology in Hip Hop Identity." She highlights the new urban language that has become a part of Rap with a locally marked lexicon, phonology, syllabic stress, consonant deletion, and vowel length.[5]

Verbal skill is the core of African American Rap. The connections of this African American performance to African oral tradition can be more clearly understood by identifying other attributes of African orature and performances. In his exploration of music and power in contemporary Africa, François Muyumba points out that Rap, in the African context, includes not only the use of more than one language, but also generic idioms or words to obscure meaning, universal principles, proverbial phrases and past historical events.[6]

In the African tradition, circumlocution or hidden messages are common devices according to Muyumba. In contrast, the message in the language is often direct in Euro-American music. Vocalization that transmits information through intonation contouring is another important characteristic of African communication and musical style. Form and rhythm are major elements in non-African music, but in African music semantics is most important. African artists avoid the direct approach. "No note is attached directly to voices; instruments often approach a note from above or below" comments Muyumba.[7]

Muyumba continues his analysis noting that Rap is ordinarily understood to represent the conversational mode. It emphasizes the individual artist's ability to outdo other artists in the conveyance of meaning without being apparent.[8] African American Rap and Hip Hop employ these same techniques.

Muyumba notes that language is important to African musicians. In Congo, the former Zaire, Lingala is a popular language because of its lexical structures, especially short-syllable words that are ideal for musical arrangements and fit in well within the time, forms, and rhythm that characterize any musical composition according to Muyumba. In African American performances, English may be the language mode, but its adaptation into special lexical structures, time sequences, forms, and rhythms speak to the African expressive traditions of African American performers.

In African American communities, this stylized rhythmic verbal expressiveness has been around for a long time. A 1940s 'soundie' or video depicted an example of an African American Rap performance called "Harlem Sings." Since the 1960s and 1970s, the term 'Rap' has become popular and the performance of Rap has gained a wide audience since the 1980s with the advent of music videos.[9]

Hubert "Rap" Brown, presented his analysis of the particular verbal rhythms and orature of some African Americans in "Street Talk," an essay in *Rappin' and Stylin' Out* edited by T. Kochman. In fact, Brown's descriptive name "Rap" expressed his own verbal skill. Rap music took on a decidedly political contour from the work of Askia Mohammad Touré and Amiri Baraka in the 1960s, later popularised by such groups as The Last Poets and

Fig. 12:   Askia Mohammad Touré, Father of the African American Word-Sound.

artist Gil Scott Heron's song, "The Revolution Will Not Be Televized."[10]

While some African American female and male performers use the Rap to vault flamboyant sexuality and materialism, this is not in keeping with the essence of African orature, which has the main purpose of enlightenment and entertainment. A number of artists connect their "Rap" to African expressive culture. They include Kool Herc, Afrika Bambaataa, Grandmaster Flash, DJ Hollywood, the Sugar Hill Gang, Sweet G., KRS One, Eric B & Rakim, Public Enemy, Davy D, Run DMC, LL Cool J, Kirtus Blow, Arrested Development, Queen Latifah, Sister Souljah and Salt-N-Pepa.[11]

It is difficult to pinpoint the founder of the modern Rap. However, Grand Master Flash & the Furious Five have definitely influenced the flourishing Rap scene. The group has been credited with creating the "Quick Mix Theory" which is the method of scratching, back spinning or "cutting up" a record.[12] According to Houston Baker's chronology, *Black Studies, Rap and the Academy*, Caribbean artists also contributed to the creative techniques of Rap and Hip Hop. In the 1970s, Kool DJ Herc, who is Jamaican, initiated the scratching technique before Grand Master Flash (Joseph Saddler).[13]

In addition to adding technical innovations, various performers have also experimented with different styles. Some performers evoke pure energy, entertainment, fun or comedy. Some examples are Tone Loc's "Funky Cold Madina,." Busta Rhymes (Trevor Tahiem Smith) teamed up with British pop musician Ozzy Osbourne in "This Means War." Will Smith's "Getting Jiggy wit it" also exemplifies energy and fun.

The performance of Rap can move beyond pure entertainment, and

Fig. 13   Afrika Bambaataa, the leader of a nonviolent organization called the Zulu Nation.

become social commentary and history as represented by the Griot.[14] The traditional Griot in West African societies challenged social transgressors to listen to the will of the ancestors. Rubie Wilkie explains that Rap is not new. Rapping is based upon story-telling. "It was passed down through generations by our ancestors. Rap music is history in the literal sense."[15]

CURRENT ISSUES – ARE RAP & HIP HOP THE SAME?

Rap and Hip Hop are used interchangeably at times and a lively debate is transpiring over the precise definition of the terms Rap and Hip Hop. Some listeners suggest that Rap can be a synonym for rhyming about anything.

Meanwhile Harry Allen of Public Enemy defines Hip Hop as a set of expressions in vocalization, instrumentation, dancing and the visual arts.[16]

Performers and audiences, however, provide varying views on the origins of Rap and Hip Hop. A New York rapper named Lovebug Starski used the term "Hip-Hop" in the phrase "chap hippity hop don't stop keep on body rock."[17] Afrika Bambaataa, the leader of a nonviolent organization called the Zulu Nation, popularized the term. Naughty By Nature retrieved the Hip Hop refrain in their performance "Hip Hop Hooray."

In *Black Studies, Rap, and the Academy*, Houston Baker notes that the Sugar

Hill Gang used the term Hip Hop as well. Their song "Rapper's Delight," became popular with the familiar lines "to the hip hop hippedy hop/You don't stop."[18] Hip Hop has accented such innovations as scratching, sampling and punch phrasing. Scratching is the sound the DJ makes with the needle on the vinyl. Sampling is using selected parts of songs recorded by other artists.

Punch phrasing is another lyrical device used in Hip Hop. Performers use punch phrases to build or anchor the Rap. Examples of punch phrasing are: performer Redman's (Reggie Noble) "I'm a hurricane Hugo and you're Miller Light Genuine Draft" or Kurupt's (Ricardo Brown) "I'm the epicenter of this natural disaster."[19]

Ultimately, however, Rubie Wilkie describes Hip Hop as an Afro-Diasporic cultural song. Hip Hop attempts to express the experiences of marginalization, brutally truncated liberty and exploitation within the cultural imperatives of African American and Caribbean traditions, personality and society.[20]

CURRENT ISSUE: IS HIP HOP AFRICAN?

Is Hip Hop African? Euro-American musicians like Blondie's Debby Harry in "The Man from Mars," the Beastie Boys and Latino 'rap' groups have adopted the Rap form and Hip Hop style. Despite the fact that Rap and Hip Hop have drawn a following from communities beyond the African diaspora, Aynda Kanyama defends the African roots of Hip Hop culture and music. Kanyama writes that Africans have used inspired musical forms that are universal in their meaning and understanding. Africans in Africa and the Diaspora use music to communicate with each other and the world. Music is used to educate, teach African philosophy and teach lessons of life. Kanyama explains that the African American musical heritage mixed "tribal" songs with a dash of Old Negro Spirituals, sprinkled with Gospel, marinated in Jazz, dipped in the Blues, and smothered in Funk. This is our newest and most controversial dish. The love child of vision and reality we call it Hip-Hop. The musical art form of the Hip-Hop generation is called rap.[21] 'Adissa The Bishop of Hip Hop' and Davy D also insist that Hip Hop is African in its essence. People of different cultures and races enjoy Rap and Hip Hop, but Adissa explains that Rap music is African oral poetry. It was transported to the Americas from "West Africa where a majority of the first so-called slaves (they were prisoners of war) were kidnapped from, Adissa writes."[22] Rap and Hip Hop have been traced through rock, jazz, the blues and gospel to their African origins.

Adissa and Davy D identify another African connection with Hip Hop. It is the element of graffiti or tagging, the art associated with Hip Hop culture. The term graffiti is supposedly of Italian origin. Euro-American archaeologists use the term, however, to identify archaeological evidence from such sites as Nekhen on the west bank of the Nile River. The depictions portray stylized, sophisticated geometric forms, parallel or isolated dashes and dots, cross-strokes and scratchings depicting animals, birds, reptiles, and plants. The graffiti has been traced to predynastic pharaonic Egypt. Scholars view these depictions as the precursors to hieroglyphs and phonetics. Ancient Egyptians used this element to express concerns and promote awareness, much like Rap artists do today. Although this may be a popular way of seeing Ancient Egyptian hieroglyphics, it nevertheless gave birth to modern writing throughout the Western world. This was a *bona fide* alphabet comprising over seven hundred signs.[23]

A variety of issues surface in conversations on Rap and Hip Hop. Listeners and performers try to pinpoint the differences between Old School and New School styles and the regional trademarks of performers. East Coast performers are said to highlight lyricism in their songs. In contrast, West Coast performers rely heavily on sampling. Southern performers have a reputation for high-energy songs and performances. But the materialism, controversial shock performances, and verbal profanity of Gangsta-rap, which have sparked a good deal of public criticism, continue to give Rap and Hip Hop culture an ominous reputation. In some cases, this reputation may be accurate. However, Rap and Hip Hop are communication forms and this chapter continues the exploration of these communication forms and their connections to African oral traditions. These traditions stress "lyrical prowess," which is the core of Rap.[24]

ANALYSIS & EXAMPLES OF RAP

An analysis of Rap reveals some of the specific techniques African and African American musicians use. One of the creative devices African musicians use is code switching. It is a tool contemporary African artists use to reach their expanding multicultural urban audiences as well as to metaphorize their messages.[25] Musician Pepe Kale Mua from Congo, formerly Zaire, can also be identified with the praise song tradition, where the voice of the soloist is always above the range of the chorus and where code switching is used as a tool for camouflaging the message. Pepe Kale mixes his lyrics' languages. He switches from Lingala to Tshiluba and Kiswahili. Zairian and Cameroonian musicians switch from French, English or an African language without loosing the power of their message.

   Pepe Kale Mua utilizes these tools in "Samuela" (chez Samuel or at Samuel's). The Rap is a camouflaged critique of the social order of deposed and deceased Mobutu's Zaire. The Tshiluba lyrics of the performance are:

> *Tuetu tuyaya*
> *Mu lutanda mua Samuela*
> *mudi tunkuasa*
> *mudi tumesa*
> *mudi tuana tua bakaji tusomba*
> *tukuma ndoshi*
>
> We are going
> In Samuel's porch

> where little chairs are
> where little tables are
> where little girls stay
> where little girls walk about[26]

Muyumba explains that the real meaning of the lyrics is hidden by the use of an impersonalized locative *mua* as the objective noun phrase and by the use of the most common, Africanized Christian name, Samuela. The artist also uses the diminutive marker *tu* as in *tunkuasa*, small tables, which generates a new meaning for "little" on the surface structure. In the underlying structure, the diminutive marker adds multiple semantic values to the word *tunkuasa* to convey the idea of small, sharp, beautiful, rich, clean, or attractive. The lyrics depict an image of a person whose life is relatively comfortable because of the alliance with the social political authority while the majority of the populace is impoverished and repressed.[27]

In the African American performance, the African technique and delivery are very prominent. Code switching, camouflaged meaning and word play are used. The devices serve the same function in both the African and African American performance. The devices communicate hidden meaning in words through metaphor and contrast.

In the song "A Perfect World" from the album *Tical 2000 Judgement Day*, Method Man (Clifford Smith) raps:

> Mr. Sandman bring them a dream
> Infra-Red lights beam
> Homicide scene
> Perfect World
> By any means get cream [money]
> Just don't let it come between you and our scene
> Everything is everything in this 3 ring circus
> People are swift trying to work us Lord
> It takes place in a world perfect

Mine, your's[28]

The word play and irony depict a world that is far from perfect. Method Man also uses cliches and historical metaphor.

Peddle to the floor
Peep the Jim Crow Law
The big apple rotten to the core
....
We're still licking the scar from
Whips on slave ships[29]

In the song "Play IV Keeps," Prodigy (Albert Johnson), from the duo Mobb Deep, known for his simplicity in style, also employs the code-switching device.[30]

Trying to form against mine
Must a just been born secluded
on a distant farm[31]

The camouflaged meaning conveys the point that it would be incredibly unwise to intrigue against his friends and family.

THE GRIOT & RAP

The role of the oral historian or *Griot* (*Djali*) has been noted in the preceding passages of this chapter. The Griot's oratorical skill is key. Muyumba writes that like the Griots of Senegal, Mali, Guinea and Benin, the Mwedi wa Kasala is a traditional historian-poet, a professional trained in history and rhetoric. Mwedi wa Kasala can recite the chronology of ruling families, critique or praise the king in public.[32]

In Senegal, Griot (or Djali) is prefixed before the given family name. Senegalese Djali D'Jimo Kouyate elaborates in "The Role of The Griot," that

Fig. 14:   Kassa Maddy, famous djali/popular singer from Kwela, Mali, the heartland of Mandinka culture, traces his ancestry to the 13th century.

it is important that people understand the roles and the power that the Griot has been endowed with since the beginning. Rubie Wilkie accents the importance of the Griot as oral historian and educator.[33]

In the tradition of the Griot and using such devices as code-switching, rhyme and semantics, Grandmaster Flash and Melle Mel used the lyrics "White lines" as social commentary. The song's lyrics "White lines, pure as the driven snow" warned about drug abuse.[34]

Some of the songs of the group Public Enemy are also reminders of the tradition of the Griot as educator and social critic. Public Enemy's lead singer, Chuck D, who is known for cutting comments on society's ills, is also known for his lyricism. He calls himself a 'wordsmith' as he raps in anger and outrage. The group members are not afraid to challenge the corporate elite and the exploitation of their performance. For example, Chuck D sued St. Ides, a manufacturer of malt liquor, for using a Public Enemy song in a commercial advertisement.[35]

The lyrics keep the focus on the Rap form. The Rap is announced with the line: "Just jam to let the rhythm run."[36] As the song continues, the lyrics and the song's title, "Revolutionary Generation" from the disc *Fear of A Black Planet*, shock and provoke the listeners to think.

Another song from *Fear of A Black Planet* is a critique of Hollywood's images of African American men.

Many intelligent Black men seemed to look uncivilized

Fig. 15.   Leader of Public Enemy, powerful artistes who make incisive commenary on African American modernity.

When on the screen
Like a guess I figure you to play
some jigaboo[37]

In "Who Stole the Soul" Rappers Big Daddy Kane and Ice Cube join Public Enemy's Shocklee, Sadler and Ridenhour in a song that deals with the politics and economics of race in the United States and South Africa.

...Ain't, no different
Than in South Africa
Over here they'll go after ya to steal your soul
Like over there they stole our gold
We choose to use their ways
And holidays notice some of them are heller days

Invented by those who never repented
For the sins within that killed my kin[38]

Public Enemy uses word play with such lexical expressions as "heller days." The rap also uses internal rhyme form "sins and kin" and ending rhyme "soul and gold."

Male rap musicians are often criticized for the use of pejorative language toward women. Admittedly the negative expressions do appear; the tone is offensive; they are used for their shock value.

In "Revolutionary Generation," however, Public Enemy's tone is soothing and complimentary toward women.

> ....Sister (hey) soul sister
> We goin' be all right
> It takes a man to take a stand
> Understand it takes a woman to make a stronger man
> (As we both get strong)[39]

Lines from the song "Fear of a Black Planet" express hope and solidarity.

> I'm here to live for the love of my people
> Kickin' it all about rebuildin' so all the children
> Avoid the self destruction...[40]

In the tradition of the Griot or Djali, Public Enemy critiques the negative aspects of life and praises that which is positive.

For the group, Intelligent Hoodlum, the word play begins with the lexical contrast in the group's name. Hoodlum is someone who is generally considered a ruffian rather than someone intelligent. But in the role of the historian-poet, Intelligent Hoodlum's verses recall in rhyme, drama, and music the history of such Black Cowboys as Cherokee Bill. The lines of "The Posse (Shoot 'Em Up)" recount that "One out every three cowboys was black." The rap describes the violence and betrayal of outlaws. Although all black cavalry units were sent west to subdue Native American nations, "The Posse (Shoot 'Em Up)," raps accurately on the commaraderie between African Americans and Native Americans.[41]

Like Mwedi wa Kasala, the Griot of Congo, who recited a chronology of ruling families, Intelligent Hoodlum recited the history of the African Americans in the West. Rap artist Common (Derek Dudley), in the song "G.O.D. (Gaining One's Definition)" is another example of a writer whose songs are intended to enlighten.[42]

THEMES, FORM & LEXICAL STRUCTURE

The preceding song texts exemplify the uses of African techniques of orature in the content, delivery and style of African American Rap. But further analysis uncovers more similarities between African expressive culture and the African diaspora. Maureen Warner-Lewis has researched the rich caché of songs brought to Trinidad by Africans of Yoruba descent.[43] She does not specifically identify these songs as 'Rap.' However, the Yoruba songs reveal the use of themes, form, lexical structure and metaphor similar to the orature found in some Rap songs.

Why did these Yoruba songs survive in Trinidad well into the 20th century? The answer lies in the particular historical experience of Trinidad, which differs from that of African Americans. In Trinidad, Africans were historically the majority of the population and it is suggested that this factor preserved distinctive African influenced speech. African languages mixed and merged with English and other European languages, but African terms survived to a greater degree than in the United States. The force of English in the US and the numerical majority of Euro-Americans, the brutal seasoning process designed to destroy African culture, made it more difficult to retain such languages as Yoruba. In the United States, the social environment and institutional repression discouraged the usage of African languages, although African speech patterns were not destroyed.

In Trinidad, however, the linguistic heritage of captured Africans took a different course. The slave trade within the British Empire ended officially in 1807 and gradual emancipation laws in the 1830s ended slavery by 1838. African labor continued to flow to Trinidad under the guise of indentured servitude. Indentured Africans in Trinidad found that their goals of quick monetary rewards and return to their African homes, were replaced by an exploitative economic system which impoverished and entrapped them in Trinidad.[44] However, Africans in Trinidad were the numerical majority and it is likely that this provided greater opportunities to use African languages despite the influence of European languages.

The songs Warner-Lewis collected from Trinidadian Yoruba portrayed themes of lament and protest over their fate. But the songs celebrated the elders and gave lessons of life through proverbs. Warner-Lewis analyzes the themes, structure, form, lexicon, metaphor and other devices of the Yoruba songs. Some are chants to the Yoruba *orisa* (orisha), while other songs are dirges that express the complexity of life and death.

Warner-Lewis analyzes the elements of African expressive traditions that remained in Trinidad. She does not explore Rap in her work. Some of the musical and oratorical devices she locates in her Yoruba texts, however, also appear in contemporary African American Rap. The following passages compare and contrast the Trinidadian Yoruba performances to those of contemporary African American artists.

The structure of the Yoruba songs includes an invitation and closing signals. The invitation begins:

É wá jádé	Come out, all
Wá wò mí o	(And) look at me

The closing signal is:

Maá lo	I'm going
Ijò mirán maá bá o sòrò	Another day I'll come to chat with you[45]

Line tags are also used. Warner-Lewis observes that a favored line tag is *o*, a sentence-final emphatic in spoken Yoruba. The term *Ayé* (world, people) functions as a mid-performance appeal to the listeners. *Ogé* (ostentation) is also very common and was probably an exclamtion inciting the dancers to indulge in their prettiest steps. *Baba* (father) occurs at line-end in some religious chants.[46]

The songs contain such structural devices as elliptical juxtapositions in which comparisons are established by the juxtaposition of ideas, without overt grammatical links between the ideas being compared.[47] Parallelism is yet another feature of the songs and lends import to the meaning, intensity and flamboyance to the song. Warner-Lewis points out that a universal syntactic pattern in oral poetry is phrasal repetition. In the Yoruba texts, binary repetition, nasal rhymes, word play and alliteration add strength and creativity to the spoken words.[48] The use of proverbs and lexical sets which signal the co-occurrence of established words and phrases are prominent as well.

African American Rap performer Mase (Mason Betha) in the song "Wanna Hurt Mase?" uses parallelism and binary rhyme in the form of a dirge.

> Wanna Hurt Mase?
>
> Chorus
>> Do you really wanna hurt Mase?
>> Or do you really wanna make me cry?
>> Or is it really that you envy Mase?
>> Or you don't really wanna see me fly?[49]

The song relays the complexity and travails of life and violence that is racially motivated.

> Now you don't wanna see me angry
> Ain't enough cops or cuffs to chain me
> Daised or raiment (arraignment)
> KKK used to hang me
> Insane me
> Ya need ice picks to hand (hang) me
> Need more than a straight jacket to restrain me
> Four more guns with my prints for you to frame me and maim me[50]

He uses the line tag 'Uh huh we like it' in many of his verses.

THE PRAISE SONG

The Kasala is the heroic praise song of the Luba people who live in the Kasai region of Congo, writes Muyumba. Similarly in the African diaspora, chants and praise songs to the *orisa* or Oludumare (Olodumare), the Yoruba supreme God (Creator) formed parts of Trinidad's expressive traditions. Whether the song was to the supreme God called *Nyame* in Akan, or *Chukwu* the God of light, the Creator or 'chi' one's personal God in Igbo, the praise song is another African song form that has carried over into Rap. Kirk Franklin's accent is on the sacred, but he used the Rap form to praise the divine blessings of God in "Stomp" by his group God's Property.

> Lately, I've been going through some things that's really got me down
> I need someone, somebody, to help me come and turn my life around
> I can't explain it
> I can't explain it
> Jesus, your love is so, it's so amazing
> It gets me high, up to the sky
> And when I think about your goodness, it makes me wanna

STOMP

> Makes me clap my hands, makes me wanna dance and

STOMP

> My brother, can't you see? I got the victory

STOMP

Salt, Cheryl James from the women's Rap group Salt-N-Pepa, continues the song.

> When I think about the goodness and the fullness of God
> Make me thankful, pit to be hateful than grateful

The Lord brought me through this far
Tryin' to be cute when I praise him
Ain't no shame in my game, God's Property
Came to get wit' Kirk, ain't no stoppin' me

No

STOMP[51]

Franklin caused a furor within some segments of the religious community. Individuals criticized "STOMP" for using a religious theme in so-called worldly music. The song text, however, was interesting not only for the Rap form. The song embodies an African concept which views the world holistically rather than neatly divided between the sacred and the secular. Secular does not, however, mean the use of profanity and obsenity.

Reverence to God and the celebration of the ancestral African kingdom of Nubia are represented by the Rap group, Brand Nubian, in their song "All for One." These are several lines of the last verse by Lord Jamar.

All your life you must teach true
Of the true and living God, not a mystery spook
And when you do that, pursue that goal
which made the student enroll, and only then you'll prosper[52]

In the same song, "All For One," Lord Jamar chants:

Rips rhymes into shape with a mic cord
I do it good cause I'm a positive black man;
You got to know the ledge of wise and dumb
And understand your culture of freedom
Power equally with the Gods
so you can build and form your cipher
All your life you must teach true
Of the true and living God, not a mystery spook[53]

The Rap, essentially a praise song form, incorporates multiple themes: a connection with God, respect for one's cultural heritage, and a quest for both wisdom and knowledge.

The praise song can also be presented as a tribute to a person. Nigerian author, Chinua Achebe, gives an example of a praise singer in his novel, *A Man of the People*. The character is nick-named Grammar-phone because of her high-powered voice. She sang praises to the Chief, the Honourable Micah A. Nanga, a politician from the fictional village of Anata. She praised his handsomeness in the following passage:

> ... perfect, sculpted beauty of a carved eagle, and his popularity which would be the envy of the proverbial traveller-to-distant-places who must not cultivate enmity on his route.[54]

Will Smith's "Daddy Loves You" used the praise song in honor of his young son. Tupac Shakur used the praise song too in tribute to his mother. In "Dear Mama," Tupac rapped:

> Even though I act crazy
> I thank the Lord that you made me[55]

Tupac's signature in the vocal delivery of the Rap is to place emphasis on the last syllable of the last word or the last word in his verses.

DMX, Earl Simmons, blends many elements of African orature and style into his Raps. He uses word play with such expressions as *It's Dark and Hell Is Hot*, the title of his ablum. DMX uses themes similar to those that Warner-Lewis finds in the Yoruba song texts: reverence for the elders, thanks for the blessings of life and the importance of the family. Simmons switches his delivery style and at times appears to be two different people. He raps loud, he raps softly. He chants slowly; he raps rapidly.

The song, "The Convo (Conversation)," is essentially a dirge. It expresses the complexity of life and death. But "The Convo" is also a praise song to DMX's grandmother, Mary Ella Holloway. Some of the song's verses contain the invitation "Ayo" to call the listeners' attention. "Uh huh" is a line tag. The song includes use of rhymes, repetition and proverbs. The song text begins:

You tell me that there's love here.
But to me it's blatant.
Nothin' but all the blood here.
I'm dealing with Satan. Plus with all the hatin'
It's hard to keep peace. (uh huh)
Thou shall not steal,
but I will to eat.
I tried doin'good, but
good's not too good for me.
Misunderstood,
why you chose the hood for me.
Mean I'm alright, (aight)
I just had to work hard at it.[36]

DMX consults his elders for guidance:

Went to gran'ma for answers,
she told me that God had it.
So now here I am,
confused and full of questions.
Am I born to lose,
or is this just a lesson.
And who it's goin' choose
when it gets turned around
And will it be
Layin' in my own blood
and on the ground.[57]

The Rap continues with a rewording of a familiar inspirational poem:

My child
I've watched you grow up
and I've been there. (un huh)

Even at those times
you least suspected it
I was there.
And look at what I've given you
a talent to rhyme.
I may not come when you call,
but I'm always on time.[58]

The next verse advises abandonment of violence and encourages faith and connection with the Creator

No!
Put down the guns
and write a new rhyme.
You'll get it all in due time.
You'll do fine.
Just have faith
cuz you mine. (uh huh)
And when you shine
It's goin' be a sight to behold.
So don't fight to be old,
or lose sight when it's cold
See that light down the road,
it's goin' guide you there
Two sets of footsteps,
I was right beside you there.

The imagery of urban violence symbolized by "the gun" and divine protection against danger are exemplified:

But what about them times I
only saw one.
Those were the times that I was

under the gun,
It was then I carried you my son.
Led you to safety.
It just wasn't your time to face me. (uh huh)

The Rap incorporates an old spiritual:

Somebody's knockin'
Should I let em in.
Lord we're just startin,
but where will it end.
Somebody's knockin'.
Should I let em in.

Another verse invokes thanks for life, his wife and child:

It was you that breathed life
into my lungs when I was born.
And it was you that let me know
what was right,
from what was wrong.
And it was you that let me know
what I knew could be done.
And it was you that gave me a good wife
and a beautiful son.
And it was you who opened my eyes
So I could see....
And it was you who shined yo'
light on me.[59]

DMX's performances merge style, charisma, good stories, catchy hooks, and one syllable words which are semantic forms used in African Rap. DMX's "Ruff Ryders Anthem" provides an example of a hook:

Stop, drop, shut 'em down
Open up shop
Oh, no
That's how Ruff Ryders roll[60]

DMX has hidden significance in elements of his performances. He barks
and he growls. According to DMX, who grew up in Yonkers, New York, a
little pit bull dog was his only friend when he was younger. In his songs, Dog
is a metaphor for friend.

Nasir 'Nas' Jones, is like a lyrical photographer. Many of his Raps take the
form of a dirge. Some of Nas's lyrics express anger over the conditions of the
Queens Bridge projects in which he lived in New York. His Raps are sometimes visionary like "Whose World Is this?" (1994). Other songs are autobiographical and loaded with metaphor and imagery. In "N Y State of Mind
II," Nas details the images of death and destruction.

Fig. 16   Nasir 'Nas' Jones

...broken glass in the hallways
bloody stained floors

Nas constructs his own lexicon in
his autobiographical verses. "Shook
of Deez" means scared of the police.
"Bid" refers to a jail sentence.[61]

In "N Y State of Mind," D J
Premier (Curtis Martin) joins Nas.
DJ Premier raps:

You read about it
You hear about it
You read about it in the Daily News.
The crime rate, the murder rate, the money rate[62]

The verse contains lexical sets, parallelism and binary repetition for

emphasis. Binary repetition, co-occurence, rhyme and parallelism are prominent in Shawn 'Jay-Z Jigga' Carter and Inga 'Foxy Brown' Marchand's hook in
"The Paper Chase."

> Gotta get that paper dog
> Gotta touch that love that paper dog
> Gotta get that paper dog
> Gotta have that grab that paper dog
> Gotta get that paper dog
> Gotta to get that spend that bend that split that get that paper dog
> I need that G-stack tell me where the G's at
> Gotta get that paper dog[63]

The verses of the hook and the entire Rap provide a ruthless uncomplimentary picture of the way business operations are set up. The paper is a
metaphor for money. The dog refers to a friend and the "G" refers to a grand
or thousands of dollars. The use of repetition and parallelism lends intensity and flamboyance to the song.

The artists on the label, No Limit, rap with pure energy. The Rappers are
loud and although the performers rap sometimes above and sometimes
below the music, the beat is at times better than the lyrics. The song, "I'm
a Soldier," is an example of No Limit's particular performance style. It is
from the album *Charge It to Da Game* by one of No Limit's artists, Vyshonn
'Silkk The Shocker' Miller.

The Rap contains some of the standard devices of other songs noted in this
chapter. Metaphor is one. The group's logo is a golden tank and the phrase
"Tank Dogs" refers to the label's artists.

Line tags are used throughout the song along with repetition of the label's
name N-O-L-I-M-I-T, which is spelled out to create effect and intensity.

Master P, Percy Miller, the label's founder, Chief Executive Officer and lead
artist, raps in a powerful, gutteral voice and identifies himself as:

> The Colonel of the tank
> People call me the ghetto E.F. Hutton[64]

Master P makes a metaphorical comparison to the prominent investment firm perhaps because he started the No Limit Record label from his own store. He now owns the successful and prolific label, real estate, gas stations, a film production company, and a sports management company that represents football Heisman trophy winner, Ricky Williams.

Silkk the Shocker, Vyshoon Miller, has a hyped staccato delivery. His use of word play is evident in his stage name. The word silk evokes something soft and luxurious while shock suggests something explosive.

Msytical (Michael Tyler), known as more of a lyricist, raps above the beat. He opens verses with punch lines to grab attention.

> One heck of ... right heah (here)
> Highly decorated lieutenant
> People don't know by now the tank can't be dented[65]

It is a song to get the listeners "crunk," meaning energetic, but some of the verses contain important themes.

For example, another artist raps:
Whooah ....
Murder murder kill kill its real
Shell shock turn your neighborhood
block into the battlefield[66]

"The battlefield" carries multiple meanings: the racial attacks and violence which destroyed black communities of Rosewood in Florida, Greenwood in Tulsa, and Oklahoma in the 1920s; urban riots in the 1960s, 1970s, 1980s and 1990s or gang violence.

The rap drifts and is picked up by female performer Mia X (Mia Young) whose strong alto pitch revitalizes the song. She identifies herself as 'Big Mama'

> We come strapped and we roll thick
> We represent the tru clique
> Playa haters yeah we know who you are
> Make infrared shine on your head like the north star[67]

The verse is full of metaphorical and hidden lexical meaning. "We come strapped" means to be prepared for whatever happens. To "roll thick" means to come to a place with a lot of people. The "tru clique" refers to the Rap group, Tru, composed of Master P, C-Murder (Corey Miller) and Silkk the Shocker. "Playa haters" refers to individuals who are envious and jealous.

"Infrared" refers to a laser, which Mia X compares to the north star. The line sets up lexical juxtaposition. The infrared has a rather negative symbol as it is used for tracking and capture, while the north star is a positive symbol. Its brightness guided enslaved ancestors running away from plantations to areas in the United States or Canada that outlawed slavery.

WOMEN & RAP

Women have made a strong presence in a musical genre which has been condemned for being anti-woman. Sylvia Robinson formed Sugar Hill Records in 1979. In September 1979, she helped propel the release of the Sugar Hill Gang's "Rapper's Delight." While it was not the first rap performed nor did it contain the best lyrics or rhyme style according to Rap music connoisseurs, "Rapper's Delight" was the first Rap song to hit the top 40 charts.[68]

MC Lyte (Lana Moorer) and Da Brat (Shawntae Harris) are among the women pioneers of Rap as well. Meanwhile Hurby Luv Bug provided the

> Yes, I'm Pep and there ain't nobody
> Like my body, yes I'm somebody
> No, I'm sorry, I'm-a rock this Mardi Gras
> Until the party ends, friends

creative spark for Salt-N-Pepa in the 1980's. But Salt, Cheryl James, Pepa, Sandi Denton and D J Spinderella, Dee Dee Roper, have become an enduring part of Rap and Hip Hop History. Verses of "Song Expression" speak of the power of woman.

Fig. 17   Salt-N-Pepa

Yes, I'm blessed, and I know who I am
I express myself on every jam
I'm not a man, but I'm in command
...I got an all-girl band[69]

The rap continues:

> Yo, excuse us while we rap
> Go ahead, girls, express yourself!
> My party, your party, anytime drop in
> Cold hip-hop is always rockin'[70]

Salt-N-Pepa's "Negro Wit' An Ego" contains a message of pride in womanhood and the African American heritage to counter the stereotype of African American inferiority.
The chorus advises:

Put some faith in your race
I'm black, and I'm proud to be an African-American soul sister
Usin' my mind as a weapon, a lethal injection[71]

The verse is an example of the heavy metaphorical imagery of Salt-N-Pepa's Raps.

Queen Latifa, Dana Owens, made her debut album, *Wrath of My Madness* in

1988. Latifa is an Arabic name which means delicate and sensitive, but her lyrics mix sensitivity with social commentary and advice. She raps:

Aspire to be a doctor or lawyer, but not a gangster.[72]

Her verses reveal complexities of life. Her father and brother worked as policemen. She has been a victim of police excesses and knows of police who have been shot.

Latifa's Raps sometimes reflect her sensitivity in the praise song, "Black Reign," in honor of her late brother. The album's title, *Unity*, recorded with rap artists of the rap group De La Soul, reflects the focus of uplift and hope.

Fig. 18   Queen Latifa, Dana Owens

Queen Latifa's recording with Monie Love takes on a slightly different theme in *All Hail the Queen* with the song "Ladies First." Latifa begins:

The Ladies will kick it, the rhyme that is wicked
Those that don't know how to be pros get evicted

Several verses later:

Who said the ladies couldn't make it, you must be blind
If you don't believe, well here, listen to this rhyme
Ladies first, there's no time to reherse

I'm divine and my mind expands throughout the universe
A female rapper with the message to send
Queen Latifah is a perfect specimen[73]

She presents the positive persona of womanhood.

Many of Lauryn Hill's Raps contain social commentary and highlight complex personal and global issues. But she uses the praise song in her Rap to her son entitled "To Zion."

Now the joy of my world is in Zion
Now the joy of my world is in Zion

Fig. 19   Lauryn Hill

...See life for you my prince has just begun
And I thank you for choosing me
To come through unto life to be
A beautiful reflection of his grace
For I could create
And I'm reminded every time I see your face[74]

The Rap performances of Salt-N-Pepa, Queen Latifa and Sister Souljah (Lisa Williamson) have tended to draw attention to issues of social, racial and gender inequities. They also celebrate the inner strength and beauty of womanhood. However, another category of female performers parade sexuality and materialism. Despite this fact their rap formats reproduce aspects of expressive oral traditions.

In her songs, Foxy Brown introduces

Fig. 20   Dr. Dre

herself as "Ill Nana." She uses word play as "ill" which can mean bad or good given the context. She uses "ill" in the positive. "Nana" is the Akan term for an elder male or female, of special importance. Female performer Charli Baltimore (Tiffany Lane) provides an example of the creativity of female rappers. Baltimore's song features a religious text, a resonant female voice and a classical piano piece in "Charli's Rap."[75] This examination of the style, delivery, content, and structure of Rap performances has identified links with Africa's expressive oral traditions. It has not included every performer nor is it a history of African American Rap and Hip Hop.

The songs range across a vast spectrum and the lyrics are sometimes brutal. But some performers rap in the tradition of the Griot with message-oriented lyrics. The delivery varies from the rapid playful staccato rapping of Bone, Thugs N Harmony to the cool 'throw your hands in the air like you just don't care' manner of Dr. Dre (Andre Young) and Snoop Dogg (Cordozar Calvin Broadus, derived possibly from Broadus, a Geechee or Gullah name). The highly provocative "2 Live Crew" (Luther Campbell and company) have shocked audiences and focused criticism on Rap for portraying hedonism and materialism which are unfortunately a part of the contemporary life.

Some of the Rap and Hip Hop artists have, however, revealed the structural elements of African orature, a part of African American communication patterns. The relevance of Rap to the Ebonics issue emerges in the song entitled "Ebonics" by the late Lamont 'Big L' Coleman. He calls his verses an Ebonics vocabulary. Verse Three contains the following examples:

> 'Ebonics'
> --Jewelry is shine.
> In love is blind
> Smiling is cheesing.
> Bleeding is leaking.
> Genuine is real
> A hard long stare is grill.
> Hotel is telly.
> Cell phone is celly.
> Jealous is jelly.

The words are English, but the rhyme and metaphor retrieve a familiar lyrical pattern in African oral traditions. African American Rap has incorporated such technological innovations as scratching and sampling. But performers have used language to create the imagery of Hip Hop: tales of myth, adventure, the problems of urban America, tragedy and inspiration.[77]

STORY TELLING, TONGUE TWISTERS & SONG GAMES

Besides Rap and Hip Hop, storytelling and song games provide additional examples of the African influence on orature in the African diaspora. Ngugi Wa Thiong'o underscores the power of storytelling in African culture. The device of personification, that is, the use of animals to demonstrate the struggle between good and evil or the forces of nature and provide lessons regarding human character, was not unique to African orature. Storytellers used image, voice inflexions and the suggestive power of language beyond their lexical meaning to develop storytelling to a high art form. While Ngugi describes his experience with storytelling as a youth in Kenya, his description applies to West Africa as well.[78] Africans brought this culture with them and it took root in African American communities.

African American storyteller, Julius Lester's "The Old King and the New King," is a farcical tale of King Junebug Jabbo Jones and the selection of a new king. Lester writes: "The other thing that's not in the story is where he did his kinging. It could've been in Zimbabwe, Zanzibar, or Zululand. Then again, he might have been king in Cambodia, Canada, or Cameroon."[79]

David Haynes, an African American folkteller, reworked the Akan tales of Anansi the spider. The tales portray Anansi in various ways, but particularly as the trickster in "Anansi Takes A Ride," "Anansi and the Turtle," and "Anansi Falls Into His Own Trap."[80] The stories are told in English, but themes and the verbal devices used are drawn from an African oral and aural tradition.

More examples of the oral tradition can be found which have made an impact on African American communication patterns. For example, Igbo poets Romanus Egudu and Donatus Nwoga write that the moonlight play was such an important cultural feature that it drew adults as well as children to the *Oboli* or *Mbala* (village square) for singing, dancing, and the reciting of riddles and tongue-twisters, as well as jocular and satirical poems.[81]

Ngugi writes of similar experiences in Kenya. He underscores that the magical power of language was reinforced by games children played with words. They recited riddles, proverbs, and transpositions of syllables in nonsensical but musically arranged words and tongue twisting alliteration. He cites a Gikuyu example:

Kaana ka Nikoora koona koora koora koora: na ko koora Koona kaana ka Nikoora koora koora.[82]

The alliteration consisted of a repetition of /k/, /r/, and /na/. The phrase means: "Nichola's child saw a baby frog and ran away: and when the baby frog saw Nichola's child it also ran away." A Gikuyu child had to use the correct tone and length of the vowel and pauses to get the verse right. Otherwise the words became a jumble of "k's," "r's," and "na's."[83]

Ghana's J. Danquah provided an Akan example that uses similar techniques of tongue-twisting alliteration.

> *Hena ko se*
> *Hena ko se*
> *Hena ko se*
> *Hena na oko see 'Te*
> *Ma 'Te ko see Ananse*
> *Ma Ananse ko see Odomankoma,*
>
> *Ma Odomankoma*
> *Boo Adee?*

The transcription for Danquah's tongue twister is:
> Who gave word,
> Who gave word,
> Who gave word?
> Who gave word to Hearing,
> For Hearing to have told Ananse,
> For Ananse to have told Odomankoma,
> For Odomankoma
> To have made the Thing?[84]

The verses are on the subject of the creation of the universe. Danquah notes that the ditty is played on the *Ntumpan* or Talking Drums, and also sung on the Speaking Horns (*Asese-ben*).

Julius Lester's retelling of "The Snake" introduces the fictional character,

Coomba. The narrator describes her as a woman who some say was from Africa. Lester uses alliterating tongue twisters in the story. The mother's code to let her daughter know that it is safe to open the door to allow the mother's entry is:

> Walla walla witto, me Noncy
> Walla walla witto, me Noncy
> Walla walla witto, me Noncy

The child sings back:

> Andolee! Andoli! Andolo![85]

Lester does not translate the little ditty. The words may even be nonsensical. But they are musically arranged and filled with repetition and alliteration.

SONG GAMES

Song games are another example of African expressive oral traditions contemporary African Americans use. Little girls sang "Jump Back Sally" or "Little Sally Walker." Toni Morrison's *Song of Solomon* is filled with metaphor, imagery and song games.

The character Milkman memorizes the rhythmic rhyming action of a round children sang which recounts the genealogy of his family.

> O Solomon don't leave me here....
> Jay the Only son of Solomon
> Come booba yalla, come
> Jake the only son of Solomon
> Come booba yalle, come booba tambee
> Whirled about and touched the sun
> Come konka yalle, come konka tambee

... Solomon and Ryna Belali Shalut
Yaruba Medina Muhammet too.
Nestor Kalina Saraka cake
Twenty-one children, the last one Jake![86]

The song games contain a number of items, which speak to an African heritage. Suleiman has sometimes been anglicized and translated as Solomon.
Belali, the name of the African relative in the song, is also the term for the
prophet Mohammad's early recruit (an Ethiopian) who was the *muezzin* (call-
ing the people to assemble for prayers). Bilal in Arabic means 'running
water.' Yaruba is one of the spellings for Yoruba. *Saraka* is Fon for receiving
blessing through offering. Morrison's passage incorporates religious expressions, the forces and elements of nature, and the entire life of the family. The
passage follows a culturally rhythmical pattern marking a cycle of birth to
death that parallels the verses of Igbo writers Romanus Egudu and Donatus
Nwoga. Their traditional verses echo the form of the Morrison text above.[87]
Song games in other parts of the African diaspora represent the African
oral tradition as well. J. D. Elder has collected a variety of song games from
Trinidad and Tobago. He describes the performance and the context of the
performance. For example, "Sambo Rainey" deals with the theme of violence, independence and self-realization. Interestingly, the name Sambo
describes an assertive male in contrast to the American stereotype of Sambo
as a docile African American male. In the song game, "Sambo" and "Bass"
(apparently boss) are characters in the enactment of a mime on the flogging
practices of slavery times.[88]

Sambo Rainey,
Bass Couner,
Da key are wo'k,
Bass Counar,
Oh lick-um till you fin' um,
Bass Counar,

Oh, lick-um till you fin' um,
Bass Counar.[89]

"Da key are wo'k" means "the key is moving." The key is a lash which is passed quickly from person to person and the searcher must find and catch the person who has it. Elder finds similarity in form between Afro-Caribbean and "American Negro game song styles."[90] He explains that the styles show a continuity of a musical tradition that is African and peculiar to all Africa-descended populations in the New World.

ENGLISH & AFRICAN SPEECH

The examples of Rap, song games, and storytelling show that aspects of African expressive culture continue to be important in the lives of Africa's descendants in the diaspora. Such critics of Ebonics as John McWhorter counter that Black English is no more of an African language than Irish English is Gaelic. In her essay, "Classroom Rap," writer A. J. Verdelle cautions that however well-intentioned the effort, "we have to assess whether ebonics returns us to a sorry place in history – whether African-American ignorance is again being written into the plan."[91]

While critics describe African American linguistic patterns or Ebonics as a collection of mistakes, Ernie Smith supports the idea of the African influence on African American speech and what he calls, the Pan-African Communication Behavior system. bell hooks elaborates on the unique quality of speech which some African Americans use. (bell hooks does not capitalize her name.) She explains: "We make our words a counter hegemonic speech, liberating ourselves in language."[92]

The supporters of Ebonics and African American vernacular do note that African descendants in the Americas incorporated their linguistic heritage into the English they were compelled to speak by their plantation owners. Lorenzo Turner's *Africanisms in Gullah Dialect* is an important document on grammatical structure, vocabulary, noun placement, and pronunciation, which Africans transferred into English.

Turner's research found that there is no distinction in form between the singular and plural of the Gullah conjugation of verbs. The verb 'to go' is conjugated:

mi go	I go
un_go	you go
i go	he goes
wi go	we go
un_ go	you go
d m go	they go.

The singular and plural forms are uninflected according to Turner.[93]

This pattern also occurs in the speech of many African Americans who are not Gullah or Guichee. Turner's fieldwork on Gullah speech revealed that verbs served multiple purposes. The verb may describe the manner of the action (mood), or character of the time (aspect), or possibly both, as they impress the Gullah speaker at the moment that is important. Accordingly, the form of the verb used to refer to present time is frequently the same as that used in reference to the past. Often there is no special form to indicate whether or not the action is continuous. In Gullah, *bin_* 'been' is placed before a verb. It may be expressed in English by the past, perfect, or pluperfect tense and the action may or may not be continuous.[94] This use of 'been' is a characteristic of African American speech in mainland communities.

The practice of using a certain form of the verb with a very general application as to the exact time of an action is common in many of the West African languages, though these languages employ a great many more forms of the verb than the Gullah dialect. According to Turner, in the Ewe language, for example, the verb is unchangeable. In Mandinka the actual time when an action takes place is of less importance than the nature of the action, that is, whether or not it is complete. In a manner similar to Ewe or

Mandinka speakers, researchers Majors and Billson note that many African Americans treat time as passing through a social space rather than a material one. Time can be recurring, personal and phenomenological.[95]

McWhorter disagrees that the roots of Black English lay in the Niger-Congo area. His research, however, contains evidence of the African linguistic influence on African American speech.

He writes that the contribution of the West African languages stayed on the level of the broad aspect of sentence structure as a whole; for example, verb-stringing, which all of the languages had in common.

Black English uses 'to be' to express linkage between two words simply by their being next to one another and as a marker of habituality. For example, 'He walking by' (right now; present tense); 'He be walkin by' (every day); or habitual (another way); 'He walk by.'[96] In Ewe, the equivalent of "is" in a sentence is optional and it may be deleted in such phrases as: *ati ko* meaning literally, "tree tall" instead of "the tree is tall."[97]

Examples of adapted 'English' communication appear in communities in Africa and the African diaspora outside of the United States. Celebrated Nigerian author Chinua Achebe incorporates the unique phrasing and grammar of English patois or pidigin in Nigeria in his writings. In the political novel, *A Man of The People*, one of Achebe's characters says to the protagonist Odili:

"Dem tell you say na gentlemanity de give other people minister...?
(Did they tell you that other people became Ministers by behaving like a gentleman?)"[98]

Another character and supporter of the charismatic but corrupt politician, Chief Nanga, says

People wey de jealous the money gorment de pay Minister no sabi say no be him one de chop am. Na so so troway. (People who are jealous of the money which the government gives the Minister do not understand that he is not the one who spends it. It's thrown away all the time).[99]

While colonialists used English to assert Great Britain's cultural suprema-
cy, some Nigerians took that language and reshaped its structure, grammar
and rhythm.

Africans transported to the Caribbean Africanized English as well. A local
Hartford, Connecticut, newspaper that the Caribbean American communi-
ty publishes, prints a weekly column "Chitchat/Chitcha" which is printed in
Jamaican patois. In one article, "Country Gal A foreign Graduation An
Ting," the narrator describes her educational opportunities:

> Dem mek me waan follow eena dem step an go learn learnings to, man.
> Me tell yuh, ma, if is one ting bout Foreign, it gi any missa man oppor-
> tunity fi go get lickle more education.[100]

In another article, the narrator reflects on the anniversary of her immigration to the United States. She encountered two children who were also going
through immigration at the airport: "All dem mussi turn big man an ooman
now. Lawks, chile, time waits for no man (or ooman) [woman]."[101] She recalls
that they have grown up into adulthood since their arrival as children in the
United States.

Examples of African linguistic influences exist in South America as well.
Within the population of Surinam, African descendants blended African languages from Ghana, Togo, Benin and the Niger area. Twi, Ewe, Yoruba, Igbo
and English mixed and produced yet another creole or patois called Sranan.
The following example reveals this linguistic blend.

> Sranan: Di Shirley doro na oso baka, en mama taki wan brifi de na a
> tafa tapu gi en.
> Literally: When Shirley come to house back her mother say a letter is
> on table top give her
> English: When Shirley got home, her mother said there was a letter for
> her on the table.[102]

According to John McWhorter's exploration of Euro-American and African linguistic traditions in the Americas, the English creole Sranan, developed by enslaved Africans in Surinam, is spoken by the whole society.

McWhorter has posed an important question: "If Black English is so African, why is it so utterly unlike creoles?"[103] Indeed the enunciation differs in Gullah, Caribbean patois and African American speech. However, similarities do exist in some instances between the speech patterns in various parts of the diaspora. Forms of the verb 'to be' are often dropped in the African, Caribbean and African American versions of adapted English. Both Gullah and Caribbean patois use 'ooman' for woman.

Elder elaborates on the speech patterns in Trinidad and Tobago's rural areas which also exist in some African American communities. The speech patterns are a mixture of English, French Creole and Spanish. The language is usually called 'broken English.' Many of the words are extremely difficult to trace to any one of the three standard languages that were at one time or other predominant in the two islands. But he notes the Pan African influence of Kikongo, Hausa, Fon, Yoruba, and Arabic on Trinidadian speech, which is found in African American communities as well. Similar to African American speech, Elder finds that the final 'd' and 'ing' are usually dropped as in 'Diamon(d) in da ring a(l)ready or "Comin(g) dung [down] with you' bunch o' roses.' Other characteristics are 'd' replaces 'th' and ommision of the initial 'a' in, for example, 'Go 'way' instead of 'Go away."[104]

Fig. 21.   Author Maureen Warner-Lewis

Muting his criticism, McWhorter finds that what is African about Black English, is the absence of 'l' and 'r' after vowels. He shows the following examples: 'stow' for store or 'co' for cold. Tone is also a feature of Black English. The recognizable melodic intonation is most likely an echo of the centrality of melody to most West African languages, says McWhorter. For example, in Yoruba, the word *fi* on a high pitch means "to dry," but *fi* means "to swing" when pronounced on a low pitch. The Yoruba word /*fo*/ with a high pitch means "to float," while *fo* on a low pitch means "to fly." Other than examples of pitch or intonation, verb stringing or the use of the verb "to be," McWhorter concludes, that the African influence in Black English is not in its structure, but in the way it is used. The call and response between orator and audience in church services, speeches, and popular music are examples of a clear inheritance from West African traditions.[105]

Linguists explore such abstruse concepts as the depth of postlexical phonological derivation in their studies of African American speech patterns, writes McWhorter. This research concentrates on the theoretical aspects of linguistics. However, much can be learned about the preservation of African languages and speech patterns among African Americans by probing documents of former slaves. Some of them continued to use African words, numerals, and sentences in Georgia and South Carolina in the 1890s according to John W. Blassingame in *The Slave Community Plantation Life in the Antebellum South*.[106]

Sound recordings of formerly enslaved men and women can be studied as well. The Federal Writers Project Administration collected thousands of these narratives in the 1930s and 1940s and at least two thousand sound recordings are available. The narratives are seering accounts of the daily horror of enslavement. But the narratives also provide examples of speech and are a rich resource for further study of the African language patterns of 20th and 21st century African Americans.[107]

AFRICAN WORDS & PHRASES
African words and linguistic traditions are active parts of African American

discourse. The preceding passages have identified grammatical constructions, vocabulary, personal names, and place names that derive from these
traditions. Although African American scholars might debate the usefulness
of Ebonics as an instructional vehicle, some are retrieving African expressions to convey their insights and celebrate a Pan-African linguistic heritage.

In his discussion of value systems, Jawanza Kunjufu uses the word *Maat*. It
is the name of an Ancient Egyptian female divinity symbolising harmony and
balance. The African American cultural celebration of Kwanzaa also incorporates African words. Kwanzaa denotes harvest, a reviewing of the past
year and preparation for the new. The core values, the seven principles called
Nguzo Saba, are: *Umoja* is unity; *Kujichagulia* is self-determination; *Ujima* is
collective work and responsibility; *Ujamaa* is cooperative economics; *Nia* is
purpose; *Kuumba* is creativity; and *Imani* is faith. Kiswahili is used because it

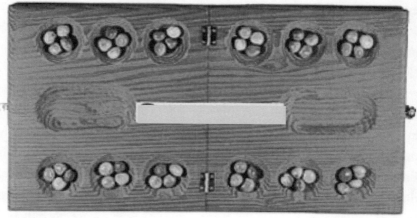

Fig. 22   African board game, wari

is a language shared by many people throughout Central, East and Southern
Africa.[108] It might be noted that Kiswahili is spoken in Congo, a region from
which Africans were captured during the slave trade.

African words remain in use in a variety of other ways. Such games as
Oware or in English "Wari" are Akan names for the popular drafts game that

some African Americans play. *Wari* is also an *Adinkra* symbol.[109] A recipe printed in a local newspaper provided the African name for the dish: "Ndiwo Za Mpiru Wotendera" (Mustard Greens with Peanut Sauce).[110]   African Americans use African words when they can whether they are used in games or recipes or in celebration.

Parts of this book explored names, grammar, and the expressive traditions of African languages African Americans use. They use English, but they have also Africanized the language with syntactical patterns and words from their own linguistic heritage.

The pattern of borrowing words from other languages is not unusual. Dictionaries of word and phrase origins identify many frequently used words in English that are actually from other languages.   Cole slaw, cookie, pit (stone or seed), boss, patroon, Yankee, caboose, spook and span (of horses) are of Dutch origin. Spaghetti, minestroni and tutti fruitti are from Italian. Such words as entrepreneur, hors'd'ouevres, reconnaissance, or attaché are French and gung-ho is Chinese.[111]

Challengers of Ebonics do not readily accept the idea that African words have been incorporated into English. Critics of Ebonics also point out that words attributed to African origins are spoken sometimes by white Americans. This is true to a degree; in fact Frederick Douglass left an important observation on this point. He wrote that white planters and their children adopted these expressions to communicate with African captives. J. L. Dillard, Molefi Asante, Roger Abrahams, and John Szwed have suggested African linguistic origins of such expressions as "OK, wow, uh-huh and unh-unh, daddy and buddy."[112] David Dalby has suggested that such expressions as OK, bogus, boogie woogie, bug, phoney, guy, dig, and fuzz are of Wolof origin. Dillard adds that while scholars debate the origins of such words as hurricane, safari (Swahili for "journey"), gorilla, chimpanzee, and banana, few would identify these words as being of English origin.[113]

Linguists dispute the African origins of certain words or phrases. For example, it is suggested that the expression "OK," *okay* from Wolof may have origins in the abbreviation of *orl kerrect* as "OK" on legal documents or the Choctaw Native American word okeh meaning "it is so."[114] The word "jig," which might be derived from the Yoruba *jigger*, was used during William Shakespeare's times in "the jig is up" for "the trick is up."[115]

African American author, Zora Neale Hurston, used the term "akimbo" in describing the gestures of one of her characters in *Mules and Men*. J.D. Elder writes that during the singing of the song game, "Miss Lucy Has Some Fine Daughters," the girls with hands "akimbo" step to the right and then to the left. The term rings of African origins though the The *American Heritage Dictionary* defines "akimbo" as an adjective and adverb which means "with the hand on the hips and the elbows bowed outward" suggesting that the word is derived from "kenebowe" from Middle English.[116] This and other words or expressions might bear further exploration however.

CONCLUSION

In the months, which have passed since Oakland school officials unintentionally made Ebonics a topic of national debate, there has been an important postscript. In May 1997, the Oakland School Board did not include the word Ebonics in their $1.95 million five year plan to expand California's Standard English Program to improve the performance of Black students who are 53 percent of Oakland's 52,000 students but post a collective grade point average of 1.8. "We do not fear the word Ebonics," said Sylvester Hodges, chairman of the Task Force on the Education of African American students.[117] The Task Force supports the Standard English Proficiency Program. Members of the Oakland Schools Task Force do not back away from the contention that teachers must be trained to assist African American students in transforming the language they speak at home to standard English.[118]

The Oakland School Board has embraced the Standard English Proficiency program in an effort to transform an instructional pattern that impeded student learning. Scholarly research proved that African American children's reading skills suffered when teachers constantly and impatiently corrected the students' speech during classroom sessions.[119]

An article in *The San Francisco Examiner* editorialized that "in the real world of colleges and commerce and communcation, it's not ok to speak Ebonics as a primary language."[120] This remark underscores the reasons for support of a teaching technique that enhances African American children's chances for success.

Theresa Perry and Lisa Delpit have edited a collection of essays in *The Real Ebonics Debate: Power Language, and the Education of African-American Children*. It records the experience of Carrie Secret who teaches English using the Standard English Proficiency Program that has several components. It respects Ebonics as the home language that stands on its own rather than as a dialectical English. It has patterns and a structure that are different from the Germanic roots of English. Students drill and practice English grammar most of the instructional time. Secret explains, "I try to connect my teaching to African proverbs, principles of Kwanzaa and the Virtues of Maat, or a piece of poetry, or recitation we are working on."[121]

The three cornerstones of the Standard English Proficiency Program are: culture, language and literacy. Research has demonstrated that college students in Chicago improved their skills in writing standard English when they were taught to translate Black English or Ebonics into standard English.[122]

The debate on Ebonics is not likely to go away and it was the prominent topic at the African American Vernacular English Conference held on September 29-30, 1998 in Athens, Georgia. Parents and scholars continue to take issue with the use of Ebonics. Some parents and educators believe that children are being taught to speak incorrectly. Other educators, for example Carolyn Temple Adger from the Center for Applied Linguistics, write that African American Vernacular English is a full-fledged dialect. Adger challenges those who support the "correct English myth" given the varied pattern of English spoken in the Euro-American community.[123]

McWhorter refers to African American communication patterns as bi-dialecticalism. He points out that bi-dialecticalism and code-switching exist in other cultures. Swiss Germans speak both High and Swiss German; Egyptians speak both standard and Egyptian Arabic; Congolese often speak standard Kiswahili and Shaba Kiswahili. Supporters of the Pan-African linguistic connection with African American orature would probably agree with McWhorter that enhancing African-American students' academic performance and general English skills are important. He does not fully embrace the concept of Ebonics, but he writes that if African American bi-dialectical competence is not a scourge or a problem, then it is something to be treasured.[124]   Indeed, African American speech patterns – Ebonics, African American Vernacular English, or Black English – are not a collection of mistakes.

This particular volume on African American communication patterns has highlighted African languages, vocabulary, syntax, grammar, expressive oral and aural forms, Rap, Hip Hop, and song games. These are the links to African Americans' Pan -African linguistic heritage. "Amelia's Song" is a powerful reminder of that enduring heritage. This dirge performed at the Tenjami 'crossing the river' funeral rite has been preserved for 200 years in the family of African Americans in rural Georgia whose relatives were among the 18th century Mende captives from southern Sierra Leone.

AMELIA'S SONG

Ah wakuh muh monuh kambay yah lee luh lay tamby
Ah wakuh muh monuh kambay yah lee luh lay kah.
Ha suh wileego seehai yuh gbangah lily
Ha suh wileego dwelin duh kwen
Ha suh wileego seehi uh kwendalyah

TRANSLATION

The grave is not yet finished; let his heart be perfectly at peace at once,
Sudden death commands everyone's attention,
Oh elders, oh heads of family
Sudden death commands everyone's attention,
Like distant drum beat
(Translation from Mende to English by Tazieff Koroma, Edward Benya and Joseph Opala.)

One of the descendants of the captives, Amelia Dawley, sang the song to Turner during his investigations. A team of researchers returned to the area in the 1990s where they encountered Dawley's daughter, Mary Moran. She had preserved the song and one of the researchers, Koroma, recognized one word as unique to a dialect of Mendi spoken in southern Sierra Leone. Mary Moran traveled to Sierra Leone with a team of researchers to see if the dirge was still part of Mendi culture. Meanwhile ,in an interior village of Senehum Ngola, they recorded a dirge by Baindu Jabati, whose grandmother had preserved a song with similar lyrics, predicting that their lost kin would return and that she would recognize them through the song. The dramatic reunion between Moran and her Mende family is the beautifully depicted in *The Language You Cry In* (Producer/Director Alvaro Toepke and Angel Serrano: Vertamae Grosvernor, Sierra Leone/Spain, 1998; newsreel.org/films/langy-ou.htm).

Notes & References

1. Toni Cook introduced the Oakland resolution, see "Opening Pandora's Box an Interview with Oakland School Board Member Toni Cook," Theresa Perry and Lisa Delpit, *The Real Ebonics Debate* (Boston, Massachusetts, Beacon Press, 1998), pp. 172-179. "Oakland Amends Ebonics Resolution," *Black Issues in Higher Education*, vol. 13, No. 25, February 6, 1997. Full text of resolution pp. 24-25. Cheryl D. Fields, "Histrionics About Ebonics 101 – What Have We Learned," *Black Issues in Higher Education*, January 23, 1997, vol. 13, No. 24, pp. 18-28. See Commentary, "Beyond Ebonics" and Randy Ross, "Why 'Black English' Matters" in *Education Week*, January 29, 1997, pp. 48, 31. Shelby Steele, "Indoctrination Isn't Teaching," ibid. Jade Pierce, "Ev'y Bodies Talkin' 'Bout Black English: Ebonics," *The Vision*, vol 17, No. 23, University of Connectcut, H. Fred Simmons African American Cultural Center, March, 1997 (Storrs, Connecticut), p. 1.

2. On the Senate hearings – ibid., p. 1: "According to the *Washington Post*, only three of the 16 members of the Senate subcommittee that oversees federal education spending attended the hearing, and two stayed only briefly. The *Post* also stated Senator Lauch Faircloth (Republican, North Carolina) denounced Ebonics as "absurd." Representative Maxine Waters (Democrat, California), chair of the Congressional Black Caucus, defended the Ebonics policy. She explained that it has been misrepresented as an attempt to lead students away from Standard English. Congressional and Senatorial debates in Washington largely focused upon spending state funds to teach Ebonics. See also Rev. Lawrence L. Reddick, III, "On Youth Currents Beneath The Ebonics Debate," *The Christian Journal*, February 1997, Hartford,

Connecticut, p. 5.

3. John R. Rickford, "Suite For Ebony and Phonics," *Discover*, December 1997, pp. 82-89. See report of Honorable Augustus F. Hawkins and statement of goal. M.C. Alleyne "Linguistic Continuity of Africa in the Caribbean," in H.J. Richards (ed.), *Topics in Afro-American Studies* (New York, Black Academy Press, 1971), pp. 119-134. Public lecture given by Salikoko Mufwene, Chair of the Department of Linguistics, University of Chicago, "Ebonics and Its African [American] Kin" with an Introduction by Marcyliena Morgan, Visiting Professor of Education, Harvard Graduate School of Education, March 31, 1998, Cambridge, Massachusetts. Perry and Delpit, *The Real Ebonics Debate*, p. 17

4. W. E. B. DuBois on metaphor of dualism or "double consciousness" as a thematic principle and psychological construct to describe the "twoness – an American, a Negro; two souls, two thoughts, two unreconciled strivings..." of African Americans who are both insiders and outsiders in US society. See W.E.B. DuBois, *The Souls of Black Folk*, (New York, Bantam Classic Edition, 1903/1989), p. 3. Perry A. Hall expounds on the metaphor of duality emphasizing the quest for freedom and literacy (historical and cultural) in "Introducing African American Studies Systematic and Thematic Principles," *Journal of Black Studies*, vol. 26, No. 6, July 1996, [pp. 713-734], pp. 717, 732-733.

5. "Oakland Amends Ebonics Resolution," *Black Issues in Higher Education*, vol. 13, No. 25, February 6, 1997 and full text of Resolution, pp. 24-25. Cheryl D. Fields, "Histrionics About Ebonics Ebonics 101 - What Have We Learned," *Black Issues in Higher Education*, January 23, 1997, vol. 13, No. 24, pp. 18-28. Ferdinand De Saussure, *Course Of General Linguistiques* (LaSalle, Illinois, Opencourt Publishing Company, 1972, 1986), pp. x, 9, 110, 191, 200. "Resolution on the Oakland Ebonics Issue Unanimously Adopted at the Annual Meeting of the Linguistic Society of America," Chicago, Illinois, January 3, 1997.

6. Ibid. Clarence Major, ed., *Black Slang: A Dictionary of Afro-American Talk*

(London, Routledge and Kegan Paul, 1971). Noam Chomsky, *Language and Mind* (New York, Harcourt Brace, Janovich, 1972).

7. John Hope Franklin and Alfred A. Moss Jr., *From Slavery to Freedom: A History of African Americans* (Boston and New York, McGraw-Hill, 1947/2000), pp. 99; 170, 181.

8. Anthony Lukas, *Common Ground: A Turbulent Decade in the Lives of Three American Families* (New York, Knopf, 1985).

9. David O. White, "Augustus Washington, Black Daguerrreotypist of Hartford," *The Connecticut Historical Society Bulletin* (Jan. 1974), v. 39, No. 1, pp. 14-19. In 1830, Hartford's black citizens opened schools for black children. Until 1852, such instructors as Augustus Washington and Ann Plato, held classes in two black churches – the North African School in the first school district operated out of the Talcott Street Congregational Church and the South African School in the second school district operated out of the African American Methodist Church on Elm Street. Washington would later emigrate to Liberia.

10. "Oakland Amends Ebonics Resolution," *Black Issues in Higher Education*, vol. 13, No. 25, February 6, 1997 and full text of Resolution, pp. 24-25.

11. Cheryl D. Fields, "Histrionics About Ebonics Ebonics 101 - What Have We Learned," *Black Issues in Higher Education*, January 23, 1997, vol. 13, No. 24, pp. 18-28.

12. Ibid.

13. Ibid.

14. Ibid.

15. Ibid. De Franz, Anita "Coming to Cultural and Linguistic Awakening: An African and African American Educational Vision" in Jean Frederickson, ed., *Reclaiming Our Voices: Bilingual Education Critical Pedagogy and Praxis* (Ontario California, California Association for Bilingual Education, 1994/1995). See http://fsweb.berry.edu/ academic/ hass/ ejohnson/eb/synops-1.txt

16. "Oakland Amends Ebonics Resolution," *Black Issues in Higher Education*, vol. 13, No. 25, February 6, 1997, p. 29-31.

17. Ibid.

18. Ibid.

19. J. L. Dillard, *Black English: Its History and Usage in the United States*, (New York Random House, 1972

_____, *Black Names*. (The Hague, Mouton, 1976).

_____, *American Talk: Where Our Words Came From* (New York, Random House, 1976). David Dalby, "The African Element in Black English," in Thomas Kochman ed., *Rappin' and Stylin' Out* (Urbana, Illinois, University of Illinois Press, 1972), pp. 170-86.

20. In New York, enslaved African American Isabella van Wagenen's first language was Dutch. When she was sold to an English-speaking family, she was forced to learn English and renamed Isabella Baumfree. She is known by the name she gave herself – Sojourner Truth. See Nell Irvin Painter, *Sojourner Truth: A Life, A Symbol*; Nellie Y. McKay, *Narrative of Sojourner Truth* (New York, Norton and Company, 1996) and *Chronicle of Higher Education*, September 13, 1996, v. XLII, No. 3, p. A18. On Cruiolo from Africa's Cape Verde Islands and the US Cape Verdeans see, Peter Duignan and L. H. Gann, *The United States and Africa, A History* (Cambridge,and New York , Cambridge University Press and Hoover Institution, 1984); on African immigration from Cape Verde, pp. 364-365. Turner cites use of Spanish by some Africans and quotes one linguist who notes the use of English linguistic "archaisms" in South Carolina and Georgia. Lorenzo D. Turner, *Africanisms in the Gullah Dialect* (Chicago, University of Illinois, 1949), pp. 9, 13. PanAfricanist and statesman, Edward Wilmot Blyden, was born in the Danish-speaking Caribbean. Edward Wilmot Blyden, *African Life and Customs* (Baltimore, Maryland, Black Classic Press, 1908). Blyden was from the Danish West Indies.

21. Turner, *Africanisms in the Gullah Dialect*, pp. 2, 13 for reference to Spanish Negroes entering South Carolina.

22. Melville J. Herkovits, *The Myth of the Negro Past* (Boston, Beacon Press, 1941/1958/ 1990) on origins of captured Africans from Senegal, Guinea,

Angola, Mozambique and Madagascar between 1786-1792, pp. 15, 27, 29, 36, 44-45, 47, 52.

23. Ben Keppel, *The Work of Democracy: Ralph Bunche, Kenneth B. Clarke, Lorraine Hansberry and the Cultural Politics of Race* (Cambridge, Massachusetts and London, Harvard University Press, 1995), p. 46.

24. Rupert Emerson, *Africa and United States Policy* (Englewood Cliffs, New Jersey, Prentice Hall, 1967), pp. 10, 52, 53. Emerson quotes Robert G. Armstrong, "Vernacular Languages and Cultures in Modern Africa," in John Spencer, *Language in Africa*, ed. (Cambridge, Cambridge University, 1963), p. 65. See also Joseph Greenberg, *The Languages of Africa* (Bloomington, Indiana, Indiana University, 1963).

25. Kwame Nkrumah, *Ghana: An Autobiography of Kwame Nkrumah* (New York, International Publishers, 1957/1981), p. 29.

26. Ibid., p. 44.

27. "Oakland Amends Ebonics Resolution," *Black Issues in Higher Education*, vol. 13, No. 25, February 6, 1997, pp. 31, .26. Full text of resolution pp. 24-25.

28. Ngugi Wa Thiong'O, *Decolonising The Mind: The Politics of Language in African Literature* (London, England, Currey; Nairobi, Kenya and Portmouth, New Hampshire Heinemann), p. 23: "Languages of Africa refused to die. They would not simply go the way of Latin to become fossils for linguistic archeology to dig up, classify, and argue about [in] international conferences. These languages, the national heritages of Africa, were kept alive by the peasantry. They saw no contradiction between speaking their own mother-tongues and belonging to a larger national or continental geography." No antagonistic contradiction existed between belonging to their immediate nationality, to their multinational state and Africa as a whole prior to the Berlin Conference, Berlin (1884-1885) drawn national boundaries. "They spoke Wolof, Hausa, Yoruba, Ibo [Igbo], Arabic, Amharic, Kiswahili, Gikuyu, Luo, Luhya, Shona, Ndebele, Kimbundu, Zulu or Lingala without this fact tearing the multinational states apart. During the anticolonial struggle, they [the peasantry] showed unlimited capacity to unite around

whatever leader or party best that most consistently articulated an anti-imperialist position. The petty bourgeoisie [African] spoke Portuguese, French, English, and [German to a degree] encouraged vertical divisions to the point of war at times."

29. Essome Keto Ebenezer, "Boundaries of Yesterday, Borders of Today and Of Tomorrow," *Afrique Histoire*, No. 1, 1982, pp. 23-26.

30. Ibid.

31. Ibid.

32. Ibid.

33. Ibid. pp. 23-26. The town is spelled Douala. The people are Duala or Dualas.

34. Emerson, *The United States and Africa*, pp. 9-10.

35. Ibid., p. 10.

36. Basil Davidson, *Modern Africa A Social & Political History* (London and New York, Longman, 1983/1992), p. 72.

37. Ibid.

38. *The Europa World Year Book 1997*, v. I, Part One: International Organizations; Part Two: Afganistan-Jordan, Europa Publications Limited, London, 1926/1997, p. 759. Cameroon Introductory Survey, "The official languages are French and English; many local languages are spoken, including Fang, Bamileke and Duala," ibid., p. 715. Adu Boahen, Jacob F. Ade Ajayi and Michael Tidy, *Topics In West African History* (Essex, England, Longman Group, 1965/1986), p. 54 on Akan clan groups and matrilineal system Bretuo clan (in Mampon, Afigyasse and Seniagya states); Oyoko clan groups Dwaben, Kokofu, Nsuta, Bekwai and Kumasi; other clan groups Asense and Ekoona.

39. J. E. Holloway, "The Origins of African-American Culture," Holloway, ed., *Africanisms In American Culture*, pp. 6-8, 15. Peter Wood, *Black Majority* (New York, Knopf, 1974), 340-341. Kathleen Kennedy Manzo, "Dr. William L. Blakey and Unearthing The African American Past," *Black Issues in Higher Education*, April 21, 1994, v. 11, No. 4, p. 14-17. David W. Dunlap and Anne Cronin, "A Black Cemetery Takes its Place in History," *The New York Times*,

Sunday, February 28, 1993, p. E5.

40. Victor Manfredi, "Sourcing African English in North America," *The International Journal of African Historical Studies*, Boston University, 1995/1996, pp. 1-20; see p. 1, figures 1 and 2). Carl Patrick Burrowes, "Some Structures of Everyday Life in Pre-Liberian Coastal Societies, 1660-1747," *Liberia Studies Journal*, v. XVIII 1993, No.2, pp. 231-244. "Broadly speaking, the people of pre-Liberia belonged to three major West African language groups: Mande, Mel, Kwa from the Kwa Coast, from the Sestos River to the Cavalla River." Ibid. pp. 232- 233.

41. *Luganda Pretraining Program Foreign Service Institute Basic Course Series*, pp. 240-243. Buganda area or modern Uganda is where Luganda is spoken [Bantu – Batazulu]. Z.C.M. Doke, M.A. D.L.H. and B.W. Vilakazt, M.D. D.L.H, *Zulu English Dictionary*, phonetics of the Zulu Language, (Witwatersrand University Press, Johannesburg, 1948); G.R. Dent and C.L.S. Nyembezi, *Scholar's Zulu Dictionary* (Pietermaritzburg, Shuter and Shooter, 1969), sounds "gq" – click sound and "gx" – click sound in ibid., pp. viii; xv. See chart of "Southerneastern Bantu Zone." Sounds of language are front and back vowels, plain consonants and clicks. Zulu is spoken in 'Zululand' and Natal, the northeastern Free State, the Southern-eastern Transvaal, Witwatersrand area. Dialectical forms are found in Ndebele in Matabelaland of Zambia (former Southern Rhodesia), in Ndebele of Transvaal, in Ngoni spoken in Malawi (former Nyasaland (particularly on the western side of the Lake) in parts of Southern Tanzania (former Tanganyika).). The dialectical forms are grouped also in the Chopi region in Mozambique, Swazi in Swaziland, Sotho in Lesotho and Xhosa (Mandela's linguistic base).

42. Alfred Burdon Ellis, *The Tshi Speaking People of the Gold Coast* (London, 1887), cited in. Holloway, "The Origins of African-American Culture," Tshi-Luba, Luba Kasai, Luba Katanga, p. 9. For Tshi-Luba (Congo) and Luba Kasai, check Winifred Vass Kellersberger in Holloway, pp. p. xii, 9 (Tshi is a River; Kasai a basin). Manfredi refers to Chiluba and Vass and Brown to Tsi-

Luba.   For Tshi-Luba (Congo) and Luba Kasai, check Winifred Vass Kellersberger in Holloway, pp. p. xii, 9. African American missionary, Althea Brown Edmiston compiled a Grammar and Dictionary of the Bakuba Language in 1932. She commented that 843 different languages were spoken in Congo and 224 of these appeared in dictionary form. She and many individuals faced the problem of distinguishing between distinct languages, dialects and other linguistic variations. See Julia Lake Kellersberger, *A Life For the Congo: The Story of Althea Brown Edmiston* (London, England, and Edinburgh, Scotland and New York, Fleming H. Revell Co, 1947), pp. 132-134.

43.   Suggested categories of language clusters are – Nilo-Saharan; Niger-Kongo; Afro-Asiatic or Kushitic-Ethiopic. Herskovits uses term Sudanic languages. See for example of Ethiopic Ayele Bekerie, *Ethiopic: An African Writing System Its History And Principles* (Lawrenceville, New Jersey/Asmara, Eritrea, 1997), pp. 82-103 on pictography, numerology, ideography, syllography, astronomy. Melville J. Herskovits, *The Myth of the Negro Past*, pp. 277-79, 281, 29, 337, 285-94; pp. 290-280. Théophile Obenga, *Ancient Egypt and Black Africa: A Student's Handbook for the Study of Ancient Egypt in Philosophy, Linguistics, and Gender Relation* (London, Karnak House , 1992), pp. 88, 117, 125.

44.   *Hausa Basic Course*, p. x. Obenga, op. cit., p. 135. John A. Umeh, *After God Is Dibia: Igbo Cosmology, Divination & Sacred Science In Nigeria* (London, Karnak House, 1997), p. 10 and Cheikh Anta Diop, *Parenté Génétique de L'Égyptien Pharanique Et Des Langues Négro-Africaines* (Dakar, Senegal, Université de Dakar, Les Nouvelles, Editions Africaines, 1977), pp. xxii, 116-117,141, 157, 184.

45.   Robert Armstrong reminds scholars that Igbo language origins cannot be studied in isolation from the origins of so-called Kwa languages from Eastern Ivory Coast to the Igbo-Ibibio border in Amadiume, *African Matriarchal Foundations*, p. 9. Connections exist in simple expressions: Fula – "baaba" and Amharic "abababba," both mean father or daddy, *Fula Basic Course*, p. 2. *Amharic Basic Course*, p. 971; *Hausa Basic Course*, "gani" means exactly but in Kiswahili a similar form appears in greetings *U hali gani?* means "How are you?" (singular), p. 12. *Yoruba Basic Course*, p. 320 and Sharifa M. Zawawi,

Ongea Converse Kiswahili (Trenton, New Jersey, Africa World Press, 1991), p. vii-ix. Elder is *mzee* in Kiswahili, the respected person is titled *nze* and an elder is *maazi* in Igbo (Ifi Amadiume, *African Matriarchal Foundations*, p. 9). Kiswahili is spoken by about fifty million in Africa from the Somali Republic, southern Sudan, Madagascar, Comoro Islands, the former Zaire, Kenya, Tanzania, Uganda, Rwanda, Burundi, northern Malawi, northern Zambia, and Msumbiji (Mozambique).

46. African writing systems and scripts are certainly ancient – Nile Valley hieroglyphic and hieratic, Vai, Amharic, Wolof, Fula, Mende, Bambun, and Kpelle. "Indeed Kubik has pointed to various pictographic, ideographic and phonological graphic systems in the region, for example among the Loma, Bambara and Dogon as well as among the Mbondo ad Ovimbundu in the central African region. He points to at least 18 graphic systems in the East and western parts of Africa exclusive of the North-Eastern cases cited earlier." Gloria Thomas-Emeagwali, "Conceptual and Methological Issues on Science and Technology in Nigerian History," in Gloria Thomas-Emeagwali, ed., *African Systems of Science Technology & Art, The Nigerian Experience* (London/Chicago, Karnak House, 1993), p. 13 [pp. 7-19]. On Adinkra symbols, see Joseph Buakye Danquah, *The Akan Doctrine of God: A Fragment of Gold Coast Ethics and Religion* (London, Frank Cass & Co. Ltd., 1968, 1944, 1968). Nine illustrations by Kofi Antubam of Achimota of Akan Adinkra symbols, frontpiece of the text, pp. 23, 35, 79, 93, 137, 138, 163, and 187; note on Adinkra [Adinkara] illustrations, pp. xxxvii-xxxviii.

47. For examples of Vai (Liberia) writing script see, Bai Tamia Moore, *Ebony Dust* (Monrovia, Liberia, Ducor Publishing House, 1962/1976), poetry in Gola and Vai, pp. 72-77. Bai Tamia Moore, "Problems of Vai Identity in terms of My Own Experience," *Liberian Studies Journal*, v. XV, No. 2, (1990), pp. 11-12. Dorith Ofri-Scheps, "Bai Tamia Moore, Poetry and Liberian Identity Offering to the Ancestors," *Liberian Studies Journal*, v. XV, No.2, poems in Vai script, p. 31; poems in Gola, ibid., pp. 32- 33. Ruth Stone, "Indigenous Invention: The Indigenous Kpelle Script in the Late Twentieth Century," on

the Kpelle Syllabary, p. 138, Fig 2, pp. 140-141. "Gbili, a paramount chief from Sanoyea, Bong County in central Liberia, invented the Kpelle script in the 1930s according to all accounts," p. 136, *Liberian Studies Journal*, v. XV, No. 2, 1990, pp. 135-144. Dalby noted indigenous scripts for the Vai, Mende, Loma, Kpelle and Bassa and possibly scripts for the Gola and Kru.

48. On Arabic as an African language, see Ngugi Wa Thiong'O, *Decolonising The Mind: The Politics of Language In African Literature* (London, England: Currey; Nairobi, Kenya and Portsmouth, New Hampshire, Heinemann, 1986/1982), pp. 6, 23, 29, 30, note #1. Ngungi writes that Arabic is now an African language unless we want to write off all the indigenous population of North Africa, Egypt, Sudan as not being Africans.

49. Boahen, Ade Ajayi and Tidy, *Topics In West African History*, pp. 85, 114. By 1880, the orthography of West African languages "reduced" the sounds to English-styled writing systems – Temne, Twi, Ga, Yoruba, Hausa, Efik. The authors cite two language groups: West Atlantic – Temne, Limba, Bullom, Sherbro, Fula, Kissi, Gola, Krim; Mande group – Mandingo or Mandinka, Mende, Koranko, Kono, Vai, Susu (or Soso) and Yalunka.

50. *Sankofa, Se wo were fi na wosan kofa a yennkyi.* 'It is no taboo to return and fetch it when you forget. You can always undo your mistakes.' *Adinkra Symbolism* (*Adinkra aduru* or *Adinkra* Medicine) prepared by Professor Ablade Glover, Artists Alliance Gallery, Omanye House, Accra, Ghana. Another meaning 'return to the past, to understand the present, to go on into the future.' On the *Sankofa Adinkra*, African burial rituals and artifacts see, Warren R. Perry, Ph.D., "Analysis of the African Burial Ground Archaeological Materials," *Update Newsletter of the African Burial Ground & Five Points Archeological Projects* (February/March 1997), vol. 2, No. 2, pp. 1,3-5, 14. Work of Dr. Sherrill D. Wilson, Dr. Michael L. Blakey on African Burial Ground Project in New York City.

51. Olaudah Equiano provides readers with insights into his kidnapping and domestic slavery in Africa. "I must acknowledge, in honor of those sable destroyers of human rights," he wrote, "that I never met with any ill treat-

ment, or saw any offered to their slaves, except tying them, when necessary, to keep them from running away." On the town Tinmah "in the most beautiful country I had yet seen in Africa." Utuma, Utu Etim or Tinan were villages on the border between Ibo and Ibibio. Acholonu identifies Equaino's father as Ichie Ekwealuo, born about 1700, and his mother as Nwansoro, from the village of Uli. Olaudah Equiano [Gustavas Vassa], *The Interesting Narrative of the Life of Olaudah Equiano* (originally published 1789), recent edition (Boston, Beford Books of St. Martin's Press, 1995), pp. 42-43, 34, 38-39, 51. John Anenechukwu Umeh, *After God is Dibia: Igbo Cosmology Healing, Divination and Sacred Science In Nigeria*, v. II (London, Karnak House, 1999), p. 8.

52. Ibid. p. 50.

53. Ibid., p. 42.

54. John W. Barber [Member of the Connecticut Historical Society], *A History of the Amistad Captives: Being a Circumstantial Account of the Capture of the Spanish Schooner Amistad, By the Africans on Board; Their Voyage, and Capture Near Long Island, New York with Biographical Sketches of Each of the Surviving Africans also, An Account of The Trials Had On Their Case, Before The District and Circuit Courts of The United States, For the District of Connecticut* (New Haven, Connecticut, E.L. & J.W. Barber, 1840) reprinted (New York, Arno Press, Inc. 1969), p. 10.

55. Barber, *A History of the Amistad Captives*, p. 10; more biographical descriptions, languages, pp. 6, 9-16, 29.

56. Ibid., p. 10

57. Egba Yoruba [Yarraba] mentioned by Martin Delany at Abeokuta, Maureen Warner-Lewis, *Guinea's Other Suns*, pp. 39, 20, 64, 54.

58. On Phillis Wheatley, A. Richmond, *Bid The Vassal Soar Interpretive Essays on the Life and Poetry of Phillis Wheatley and George Moses Horton* (Washington, D.C., Howard University Press, 1974), pp. 3-63.

59. Broteer Furro, Venture Smith, *A Narrative of the Life and Adventures of Venture A Native of Africa But a Resident Above Sixty Years in the United States of America Related By Himself* (New London, Connecticut, 1798; Middletown,

Connecticut, J.S. Stewart, Printer and Bookbinder, 1897) in Arna Bontemps, ed., *Five Black Lives* (Middletown, Wesleyan University Press, 1971), pp. 4-10.
60. Abd-ar-Rahman, *Rev. Thomas H. Gaullaudet, A Statement with regard to the Moorish Prince, Abduhl Rahahman* (New York, 1828). He had been a military commander in Timbo, p. 38. The Prince remained a Muslim, returned to Africa with the aide of the Colonization Society and died in Liberia. Before leaving the U S, he so met John Q. Adams. "By the 1700s, when large numbers of African Muslims including members of the Hausa, Mandingo [Mandinka], and Fulani peoples – were being made victims of the translatic slave trade, Islam had a thousand-year history in West Africa." "America's First Black Muslims," *American Legacy,* Winter 1998, v. 4/No. 4, p. 33.
61. Yarrow Mamout, ibid., p. 34.
62. Job Ben Solomon, op. cit., p. 36.
63. Omar ibn Sayyid, Ibid., p. 36.
64. On Betsey Bailey, Stuckey, *Going Through the Storm*, pp. 33-36.
65.   Frederick Douglass, *Autobiographies: My Bondage and My Freedom, Narrative of the Life of Frederick Douglass, The Life and Times of Frederick Douglass* (NewYork: The Library of   America, 1984), pp. 168-169.
66. Douglass, *My Bondage and My Freedom*, p. 476. Stuckey, *Going Through The Storm*, pp. 50, 151, 168. Dillard, *Black English*, p. 119 .
67. Major, *Juba To Jive*, p. 481.
68. Wilson Jeremiah Moses, *Alexander Crummell: A Study of Civilization and Discontent* (New York, Oxford University Press, 1989). Stuckey cites James Fenimore Cooper's *Santanstoe*, published in 1845, pp. 122-123. James Fenimore Cooper, *Santanstoe or The Littlepage Manuscripts A Tale Of The Colony* (New York, Hurd and Houghton and Cambridge, Riverside Press, 1972), pp. 63-79, 84. Major, *Juba to Jive*, Pinkster Day, (1750s-1860s), p. 352.
69. On the arrival of the last slave ships, Turner, *Africanisms in Gullah Dialect*, p. 1, notes that 420 Africans landed in 1858 Brunswick, Georgia. W. Kellersberger Vass, *The Bantu-Speaking Heritage of The United States*, p. 17. Between 1811 and 1861, slave traders brought African captives into the United

States. Duignan and Gann, *The United States And Africa: A History*, pp. 366-367, 376; Holloway, p. 112.   Daniel P. Mannix and Malcolm Cowley, *Black Cargoes: A History of the Atlantic Slave Trade*, 1518-1865 (New York, Viking Press, 1962), pp. 203-5.   Warren S. Howard, *American Slavers and the Federal Law, 1837-1862* (Berkeley, University of California Press, 1963).   Philip D. Curtin, *The Atlantic Slave Trade, A Census* (Madison, University of Wisconsin Press, 1939).   David Eltis, Stephen D. Behrendt, David Richardson and Herbert S. Klein, "The Transatlantic Slave Trade, 1527-1867," A Database Prepared at the W.E.B. DuBois Institute at Harvard University, April 25-26, 1998.

70. W.E. Burghardt DuBois, *Darkwater Voices From Within The Veil* (New York, Harcourt, Brace And Howe, 1920), p. 5.

71. W.E. B. DuBois, *Dusk of Dawn* (New York, 1940), p. 114. Sterling Stuckey, op. cit., p. 128 on Pinkster, pp. 58-80.

72. W.E. Burghardt DuBois, *Darkwater Voices From Within The Veil* (New York, Harcourt, Brace And Howe, 1920), pp. 5, 7, 11.

73. Carl T. Rowan, ed., *Dream Makers, Dream Breakers The World of Thurgood Marshall* (Boston, Little, Brown and Company), p. 34.

74. Charles Henry, ed., *Selected Speeches and Writings of Ralph Bunche* (Ann Arbor, Michigan, University of Michigan Press, 1998/1995), p. 320.

75. Ibid.

76. Ibid., p. 120. 76. Keppel, *The Work of Democracy: Ralph Bunche, Kenneth B. Clark, Lorraine Hansberry*, p. 42.

77. Ibid., p. 42.

78. De Franz, Anita "Coming to Cultural and Linguistic Awakening: An African and African American Educational Vision' in Jean Frederickson, ed., *Reclaiming Our Voices: Bilingual Education Critical Pedagogy and Praxis* (Ontario, California, California Association for Bilingual Education,1994/1995). See http://fsweb.berry.edu/ academic/hass/ejohnson/eb/ synops-1.txt.

CHAPTER II

1. On *chi* and *ka*, see Ifi Amadiume, *African Matriarchal Foundations, The Case of Igbo Societies*, p. 9. On 'soul' see Major, *Juba to Jive*, pp. 434-436. Mashona - on *ka, chi, na*: on the *ka* tense, *Shona Basic Course*, pp. vi, 51; use of the connective *na* with personal pronouns, pp. 177-184; use of the *chi* participial form in "why" questions, pp. x, 227-237; use of *chi* in imperative forms, pp. xiii, 346-354. Linguists Mr. and Mrs. Matthew Mataranyika, Earl W. Stevick, Gabriel Cordova, *Shona Basic Course* (Foreign Service Institute, Department of State, Washington, D.C., 1965). On the writing system and transcription of Igbo (Niger-Congo language cluster) see Lloyd Swift, Amako Ahaghota and Chidiadi Ugorji, *Igbo Basic Course* (Washington, D.C. Foreign Service Institute, Department of State, 1962), pp. iii, 3-55.

2. Danquah, *The Akan Doctrine of God A Fragment of Gold Coast Ethics and Religion*, p. xxxvii on 'soul.' *okra* or *okara*. The word *nkra* or *nkara* means message, intelligence, and where human destiny or the life span is concerned, it refers particularly to the intelligence or message which each soul takes with him from God upon his obtaining leave to depart to the earth... *Adinkra* cloth and symbols intended to mark the link forged between living and dead, present and future, affairs of now and the hereafter.

3. Ibid., pp. xxix, xxix, 44, 45.

4. Ishmael Reed, *Mumbo Jumbo, A Novel*, (New York, Atheneum/Macmillan Publishing Company, 1972/1988), pp. 7, 24-25.

5. Mumbojumbo – [Mandingo *ma-ma-gyo-mbo*, "magician who makes the troubled spirts of ancestors go away": *ma-ma*, grandmother + *gyo*, trouble + *mbo*, to leave] *The American Heritage Dictionary of the English Language* in Reed, *Mumbo Jumbo*, p. 7. See also "mumbo jumbo, meaningless incantation or ritual. Rhyming alter of Mandingo [Mandinka] Mama Dyumbo a tribal god," *The Random House Dictionary of the English Language College Edition* (Random House, New York, 1950/1968), p. 877. *The American Heritage Dictionary*, Second College Edition (Boston, Massachusetts, Houghton Mifflin Co., 1982/1985), p. 822.

6. Gullah and Guichee (Geechee); in Major, *Juba to Jive*, p. 216. Gullah African Americans of coastal Georgia and South Carolina; Turner, *Africanisms in the Gullah Dialect*, pp. 15-30; 209-222.

7. Joseph E. Holloway and Winifred K. Vass, *The African Heritage of American English* (Bloomington, Indiana, Indiana University Press, 1993). Victor Manfredi, "Sourcing African English in North America," *The International Journal of African Historical Studies*, Boston University, 1995/1996, [pp. 1-20], pp. 11, 12, 14. Turner, *Africanisms in the Gullah Dialect*, Demba [Mandinka] name given the third son, p. 73. Turner wrote down this dirge preserved for 200 years in the family of African Americans in rural Georgia whose relatives were among the 18th century Mende (Mendi) captives from southern Sierra Leone. The dirge or hymn is usually performed at the Tenjami 'crossing the river' ceremony during burial rites. Alvaro Toepke and Angel Serrano, Sierra Leone/Spain,"The Language You Cry In, The Story of a Mende Song" (1998), and www. newsreel.org/films/langyou.htm

AMELIA'S SONG

Ah wakuh muh monuh kambay yah lee luh lay tamby
Ah wakuh muh monuh kambay yah lee luh lay kah.
Ha suh wileego seehai yuh gbangah lily
Ha suh wileego dwelin duh kwen
Ha suh wileego seehi uh kwendalyah

Translation from Mende [Mendi] to English by Tazieff Koroma, Edward Benya and Joseph Opala:

The grave is not yet finished; let his heart be perfectly at peace.
Every one come together, let us work hard:
The grave is not yet finished; let his heart be at peace at once,
Sudden death commands everyone's attention,
Oh elders, oh heads of family
Sudden death commands everyone's attention,
Like distant drum beat

8. Turner, op. cit., pp. 1- 2 on origins of slaves in South Carolina and Georgia,and Vocabulary list, pp. 43, 208.

9. Ibid., p. 243 on Yoruba, Hausa and Ibibio in Turner's table of languages.

10. Ibid., p. 245. Turner pointed out that English people in the Shetland and Orkney Isles, Pembroke, Kent and Sussex also pronouce such words as: this, that and them as *dis, dat* and *dem*.

11. *The American Heritage Dictionary Second College Edition*, p. 27.

12. Turner, *Africanisms in Gullah Dialect*, p. 105 on examples are Kano and Abomey.

13. Julie Dash, "Daughters of The Dust," Geechee Girls Production (1991). Molefi Kete Asante, "African Elements In African American English," in Holloway, ed., *Africanisms in American Culture*, p. 19.

14. Cape Verdean Cruiolo, Cape Verde, Duignan and Gann, *The United States and Africa: A History*, pp. 364-365. Cape Verdeans came in several waves. Records indicate that they arrived, in some cases, voluntarily as early as 1778 in New England. Some Cape Verdeans are of Portuguese descent, some of African descent and others have African and Portuguese parentage. "Dark-skinned Cape Verdeans were known as black Portuguese, although they spoke a distinctive form of Portuguese known as Crioulo." By the 1970s, it was estimated that there were three hundred thousand. Rhode Island in fact formed a bilingual education department that also looked after Cape Verdeans' needs. Communities exist across the US as far as Ohio, Scramento, California, strongholds are Rhode Island, Nantucket Island, Bridgeport and New Haven, Connecticut.

15. Papiamento is a fusion of Dutch, Portuguese, Spanish, and African languages spoken in Curacao, Aruba and the Dutch Antilles. Maureen Warner-Lewis, *Guinea's Other Suns The African Dynamic in Trinidad Culture* (Dover, Massachusetts, The Majority Press, 1991), pp. 2-6. *Dictionnaire Pratique du Creole de Guadelope suivi d'un index francais-creole*, by Henry Tourneux and Maurice Barbotin (Karthala – ACCT, Marie-Galante, Paris, 1990).

16. Danquah, *The Akan Doctrine of God*, pp. 47-48.

17. Ibid., pp. 47-48.

18. Dillard, *Black English*, p. 124.

19. Blassingame and Berry, *Long Memory*, p. 19; Osepetetreku Kwame Osei, *The Ancient Egyptian Origins of the English Language* (Trans Atlantic International, New York and Accra, Ghana, Camden Graphics, 1996), p. 29.

20. Blassingame and Berry, *Long Memory*, Ibid., p. 19. Missionaries did not accurately transcribe sounds of the Akan language and anglicized spellings – Ashante instead of Ashanti, Twe instead of Twi, Fante instead of Fanti and Qu instead of Kw. See also Osei, op.. cit., p. 29 on Adi - Addy or Adie Addison Adi's son.   Sheldon H. Harris, *Paul Cuffe: Black America and the African Return* (New York, Simon and Schuster, 1972).   Note the anglicized spelling of Cuffe's name instead of Kofi.

21. Blassingame and Berry, op. cit., p. 19. Ogundipe Fayomi, *Names – Layout and Illustration Afrikan Names, Why, Which, What, Where* (Brooklyn, New York, East Distribution and Publication, 1974): Yoruba, Titi, flower, p. 12; Nini, pp. 5, 11; Dorcas, (East. Africa) p. 8; Mariama (Guinea and Ivory Coast), p. 13; Kwasi and Kwesi, p. 6; *Chaka* (Great King), p. 9; *Nana*, Mother of the Earth, p. 5.

22. On the name Juba, Major, *Juba To Jive*, p. 263.

23. Robert M. Maxon, *East Africa: An Introductory History* (Morgantown, West Virginia, West Virginia University) on Juba and on Jubaland, pp.158-159.

24. Dillard, *Black English*, pp. 130-31.

25. On the name Sambo, Major, op. cit., p. 396.

26. On Sambo, Berry and Blassingame, op. cit., pp.75, 300. See also *Fula Basic Course*, Samba, a name, p. 31; Turner, op. cit., p. 155 on Sabo and Samba. Dillard, *Black English*, p. 131.   Stanley M. Elkins constructed the Sambo stereotype in *Slavery, A Problem In American Institutional and Intellectual Life* (Chicago, University of Chicago, 1976), pp. 13, 82.

27. Dillard, op. cit., p. 130, on the complexity of names or terms in African languages, lexical tones and pitch convey varied meanings though spelling may be the same. See Turner cited by Dillard, "Sambo" a Hausa name given

to the second son in the family; in Mende and Vai "Sambo" can mean disgrace or misfortune; Mende-Hausa-Vai differentiated in the pronunciation. On the name Sambo, see Major, op. cit., *Fula Basic Course*, Samba, a name, p. 31.

28. Dillard, op cit., pp. 124, 125.

29. On Nana - Danquah, op. cit., p. xxix. Nana Prempeh I of Asante (1873-1931) and Nana Yaa Asantewa, Queen of Edweso and leader of the 1900 Asante Rebellion.

30. Danquah, *The Akan Doctrine of God*, p. xxix. On Nana, see Turner, op. cit., p. 135.

31. Ralph J. Bunche called his maternal grandmother, Lucy Johnson, 'Nana' in Henry, *Ralph J. Bunche*, p. 2. Warner –Lewis, *Guinea's Other Suns*, p. 66: Na, Nana. Kwame Anthony Appiah, *In My Father's House Africa: in the Philosophy of Culture* (New York, Oxford University Press, 1992/1993), pp. 181, 182, 190. Appiah describes the description of events surrounding his father's funeral and the importance of his father's matriclan, the abusua, the Ekuona clan.

32. These words are identified by Turner –' lir and fa'.

33. Turner, op. cit. p. 46 *ago'go*, a bell in Gullah.

34. An African American children's song contains the lyrics 'Way down yonder in the paw paw patch.'

35. Ñallen jam, *Fula Basic Course*, p. 23.

36. Earl w. Stevick, Olayeye Aremu, Josiah Simaren, Alexander Edwards, and Samuel Adebonojo, *Yoruba Basic Course* (Washington, D.C., Foreign Service Institute, 1963), pp. 319-320.

37. Ibid. on *jiga, bi, da*.

38. *Yoruba Basic Grammar*, pp. 314, 326. T. Ajayi Thomas, *History of Juju Music: A History of An African Popular Music from Nigeria* (Jamaica, New York, The Organization, 1992). Christopher Waterman, *JuJu: A Social History and Ethnography of an African Popular Music* (Chicago, University of Chicago, 1990), pp. xi, 73. Jújù, though Yoruba based, incorporated Kru, Ashanti, Ewe, and Fanti languages. Waterman points out that missionaries and linguists

established Yoruba orthography in an attempt to reproduce nazalization, pitch glides, and timbral effects in tone.

39. *Yoruba Basic Grammar*, pp. 63, 105; 326, 354. Joseph Ajayi Fashagba, *The First Illustrated Yoruba Dictionary* in two parts Yoruba-English and English-Yoruba (Toronto, Canada, 1991). Major, *Juba To Jive*, p. 259.

40. Ibid., p. 254 on Tshiluba.

41. Major, op.cit., p. 516.

42. Ibid., jito-bag,

43. Major, op. cit., p. 516.

44. Wolof *jama*, jamboree, Major, op. cit., pp. 254, 217, 258.

45. *Wolof Grammar*, p. 85 "def" to do; Major, op. cit., p. 132.

46. "Def" in Major, op. cit., p. 132

47. Comedy show sponsored by Russell Simmons who owns Def Jam Entertainment, the largest black American record label with clothing and promotions operations as well.

48. *Wolof Grammar*, "Da" (or "Dafa") in Wolof meaning 'it' is an explicative predicator. For example: *Da nga mun(-a) naan lool.* "It is that you drink" too much or "You drink too much," p. 52

49. Turner, op. cit., p. 245. He points out that 'da,' 'de,'appears frequently in African language constructions.

50. They often lacked "th" sound and Africans transfered the familiar sound "da" or "de" to use as a substitute. Turner, op. cit., p. 245.

51. Wolof also includes *Bii, Bee* which were confused with the English verb root "to be". In Wolof, *Bii, Bee*, functions as "you", a noun determiner to express distance.

52. Dillard, op. cit., p. 119. Major, op. cit., pp. 230, 234.

53. Major, op. cit., p. 259.

54. Ibid., p. 264.

55. *Wolof Grammar*, pp. 19, 51

56. Ibid., pp.19, 51.

57. Ibid., pp. 68, 17.

58. F. G. Cassidy and R.B. LePage, *Dictionary of Jamaican English*, (London, Cambridge Cambridge University Press, and Binghamton, New York, Vail-Ballou Press, Inc., 1967/1980), pp. 131 256.

59. Osepetetreku Kwame Osei, op. cit., p. 91.

60. Ibid., p. 63.

61. Ibid., p. 63.

62. Ibid., p. 102.

63. Ibid., p. 62.

64. Ibid., p. 80.

65. Cassidy and LePage, op. cit., p.18.

66. Joseph T. Shipley, *The Origins of English Words A Discussive Dictionary of Indo-European Roots* (Johns Hopkins University Press, Baltimore/London, 1984), p. 155 .

67. Mojo charm from *muoyo* meaning "life"; Mojo http:/1www.sonic.net/% 7Eyronwode mojo.html Jim Morrison "Mojo rising "My Mojo Risin"; Muddy Waters (McKinley Morganfield).

68. The Stylistics "Betcha By Gooly."

69. Major, op. cit., p. 516.

70. Vass, *The Bantu Speaking Heritage*, p. 54. Members of the Creek Nation who left Georgia and moved to Florida called themselves 'siminoli' meaning runaway. Enslaved Africans who fled plantations and found sanctuary among the Siminoli also used the name. The name was anglicized and spelled Seminole. See *Indians of North America Series – Seminole*, Schlesinger Video, Invision Comm Inc. Bala Cynwyd, Pennsylvania, 1993.

71. Vass, op. cit., pp. 54, 55, 59. *Rand McNally Road Atlas*, pp. 74, 123, 125, 126. Manfredi, "Sourcing," p. 14.

73. Vass, op. cit., pp. 52, 53. *Rand McNally Road Atlas*, p. 122.

74. Ibid., pp. 29, 46, 47. *Rand McNally Road Atlas*, p. 119. *Georgia/Alabama Map* (American Automobile Association, 1993).

75. Vass, op. cit., pp. 44, 45, 50, *Rand McNally Road Atlas*, p. 118, 119. *Georgia/Alabama Map*.

76. Vass, op. cit., p. 31. *Rand McNally Road Atlas*, p. 119.

77. A 1932 dictionary of "Bantu" words published by African American Althea Brown Edminston translations of African words. Kellersberger, *A Life For the Congo*, pp. 32-134

78. Vass, op. cit., "Chumukla," pp. 49, 43, 52.

79. Positive: Υ_- *re ko*.   Negative: Υ_- *re n ko*
                   We are going.   We are not going.

   Osei, op. cit., p. 86

80. The places appear on local city maps.

81. *Dem* is a verb in Wolof meaning to "leave," for example, *Mangi dem na kër*. "I am leaving [to go] home. *Wolof Grammar.*, p. 42   Carleton T. Hodge and Ibrahim Umaru, *Hausa Basic Course* (Washington, D.C., Foreign Service, Institute, 1963), pp. xv, 38, 187, 166.

82. Osei, op. cit., p. 86.

83. *Wolof Grammar*, p. 42.

84. *Hausa Basic Course*, pp. 166-168.

85. Virginia Hamilton (illustrated by Leo & Diane Dillon), *Her Stories -African American Folktales, Fairy Tales, and True Tales* (New York: The Blue Sky Press, 1995), p. 41

86. Ibid., p. 41.

87. Ibid., p. 39 "Mom Bet And The Little Ones A-Glowing," pp. 39-40.

88. Ibid.,p. 40.

89. Ibid., p. 37. "There are several mermaid tales that originated in the communities of the Cape Verde Islands off the African coast."

90. Jamal Koram the Story Mann, "The Lion And The Ashiko Drum, A Fable From South Carolina," Linda Goss and Marian E. Barnes in Henry Louis Gates, ed., *Talk That Talk: An Anthology of African American Storytelling* (New York, Simon and Schuster/Touchstone), pp. 244-246.

91. Frankie and Doug Quimby as told to Marian E. Barnes, "The Ibo [Igbo] Landing Story," story of Africans, Igbo who were tricked, shipped to St. Simon's Island on the east coast of Georgia, found out they were going to be

sold as slaves, drowned themselves in Dunbar Creek, in Goss, *Talk That Talk*, pp. 139-140.

92. Blassingame and Berry, *Long Memory*, pp. 17, 18, 21, 75. Fortier, Alcee, collector and ed., *Louisiana Folk-Tales in French Dialect and English translation* (Boston, 1895) in Blassingame and Berry.

93. Goss and Barnes, op. cit., p. 25.

94. William J. Faulkner, "Brer Tiger And The Big Wind," Ibid., pp. 25-28.; pp. 39 - 41.

95. Louise Bennett, "Anancy An Him Story, A Tale From Jamaica," ibid., pp.39-41, adapted and retold by Marian E. Barnes; "Anansi's Riding Horse, A Jamaican Folktale," ibid., pp. 42-44.

CHAPTER III

1. Richard Majors and Janet Mancini Billson, *Cool Pose The Dilemmas of Black Manhood In America* (Lexington Books, New York, 1992), pp. 55, 9.

2. Ibid., pp. 55-56.

3. W. Boykins, "The Academic Performance of Afro-American Children," in J. Spence, ed., *Achievement and Achievement Motives* (San Francisco, W.H. Freeman, 1983); Majors and Billson, op. cit., pp. 57, 91. C. Majors, *Juba To Jive*, pp. 376-377.

4. Majors and Billson, op cit., pp. 92, 93, 95.

5. Marcyliena Morgan, "Ain't nothin' but a G thang': Grammar, Variation and Language Ideology in Hip Hop Identity," African American Vernacular English Conference with original papers September 29-30, 1998, Athens, Georgia. http://dir.yahoo.com/ Society_ and_ Culture/Cultures _and_ Groups/Cultures/ American_.../Ebonics.

6. François N. Muyumba, "Music and Power in Contemporary Africa:

Language and Expressivity," *The Literary Griot*, 5. 1, Spring 1993, pp. [50-67], 51, 54.

7. Ibid., p. 51.

8. Ibid.

9. Majors and Billson, op. cit., pp. 93, 95. Major, *Juba To Jive*, pp. 376-377.

10. H. Rap Brown, 1972, "Street Talk" in T. Kochman, ed., *Rappin' and Stylin' Out*, pp. 205–208 (Urbana, University of Illinois Press, 1972); Majors and Billson, op. cit., pp. 25-27.

11. Rubie Wilkie, "Rap Music," *The AFRIKAN*, 2nd Issue 1996-1997, p. 30.

12. Grandmaster Flash,http://www.wbls.com/dj_ folder/dj_gmflash.html.

13. Earleen De La Perriere and Earl Ingersoll, "Rap: The Critical Challenge of Houston A. Baker," *The Literary Griot*, 5. 1, 1993, p. 71 and Houston A. Baker, *Black Studies, Rap and the Academy* (Chicago, University of Chicago, 1993).

14. Rubie Wilkie, "Rap Music," *The AFRIKAN*, 2nd Issue 1996-1997, p. 30.

15. Ibid.

16. Hip Hop Culture and the Internet: Expansion or Exploitation? by Allen Burnett-Film176c- Margret Morse http://www.mrblunt.com/culture/hh_net.html

17. Jawanza Kunjufu, *Hip-Hop vs. MAAT: A Psycho/Social Analysis of Values*, (Chicago, Illinois, African American Images, 1993) p. II. Naughty By Nature's members Vinnie, Treach and Kay Gee.

18. La Perriere and Ingersoll, op. cit., pp. 68, 71. http;//yomama.bus. miami. edu/l douglas/house/shill/

19. Pete Rock (producer/rapper) "Tru Master" feat Inspektah Deck and Kurupt.

20. Rubie Wilkie, op. cit. Erick Sermon and Parrish Smith of EPMD were a leading Hip-hop duo in the 1980s and early 1990s.http://www.mrblunt. com/culture/history.html. Jawanza Kunjufu, op. cit., p. II.

21. http://www.mrblunt.com/culture/hiphopfrom the roots.html. Hip Hop Essays by Davey D; "Hip-Hop From The Roots" by Aynda Kanyama.

22. "A Response: Hip Hop Is Indeed Black Culture" by Adissa The Bishop of Hip Hop http://www.mrblunt.com/culture/blk_hiphop2

23. "Origins Of The Elements, " http://www.mrblunt.com/culture/origin. html by Da%2oRuTKuS@aol.com.   Walter Fairservis, *The Hierakonpolis Project, The Graffiti Origins of Egyptian Hieroglyphic Writing*, Number II, (Poughkeepsie, New York, Vassar College, 1978) pp. 1-10, 22-28. William S. Arnett, *The Predynastic Origins of the Egyptian Hieroglyphs*. (Washington, D.C., University Press of America, 1982), pp. 5, 10-11, 23-25, 31-44. A. H. Gardiner, *Egyptian Grammar* (Oxford, Clarendon Press, 1927), p. 19.

24. http://www.mrblunt.com/culture/history.html

25. François N. Muyumba, "Music and Power in Contemporary Africa: Language and Expressivity," *The Literary Griot*, 5. 1, Spring 1993, pp. 50-67.

26. Ibid., p. 55.

27. Ibid., pp. 55-56, 66.

28. Method Man, Clifford Smith, *Tical 2000 Judgment Day*, "A Perfect World," Method Man from the Rap group Wu Tang Clan.

29. Ibid.

30. Mobb Deep and Prodigy [Albert Johnson] "Play IV Keeps."

31. Ibid.

32. Muyumba, op. cit, p. 66.

33. D'Jimo Kouyate, Senegalese Griot "The Role of The Griot," in Linda Goss and Marian E. Barnes, eds., *Talk That Talk An Anthology of African American Storytelling*, pp. 179–181.

34. Rapper's Delight, White Lines Don't Don't Do It, The Message on 'The Showdown The Sugarhill Gang vs. Grandmaster Flash & The Furious Five" by Grandmaster Flash and Melle Mel. See also the songs of Curtis Blow recorded between 1979 and 1982.

35. "Beats, Booze, and Blunts: Drugs In the Rap Industry," Hip Hop Culture and the Internet: Expansion or Exploitation? by Allen Burnett-Film 176c-Margret Morse.Armoudian, Maris. 1994. "Beating the Bad Rap," *Billboard*. 106.48: 48. Smith, Danyel. 1994. Ryan W. Waxenberg, "Positively P.E.,"

Rolling Stone, 685:30 (1995).   The Do-Boy Productions Compilation: 1993-1995. C. Smith, Dallas: Do-Boy Productions (1995).   "Headbanger Boogie," The Show: The Soundtrack. New York: Def Jam Music Group, Inc. Andre Young, "The Chronic," Dr. Dre. Los Angeles: Interscope Records (1992).

36. Public Enemy. http://www.publicenemy.com/archives/lyrics/index.html.

37. Ibid., lyrics/index.html

38. Album, *Fear of a Black Planet* from 'Who Stole the Soul' (Shocklee-Sadler-Ridenhour) also Big Daddy Kane and Ice Cube.http:// www. public enemy.com /archives/lyrics/index.html

39. Public Enemy. http://www.publicenemy.com/archives/ lyrics/index.html

40. Ibid.

41. Intelligent Hoodlum, 'The Posse (Shoot 'Em Up)' from the soundtrack Posse, 1993.

42. Muyumba, op. cit., p. 66.

43. Warner-Lewis, *Guinea's Other Suns*, pp. 53-56, 79, 80, 82,

44. Ibid., pp. 61-79, 82, 83, 87.

45. Ibid.

46. Ibid.

47. Ibid.

48. Ibid., pp. 102, 104 107, 108.

49. http://wwnet.fi/users/llcooj/wannahurtmase.htm

50. Ibid.

51. Muyumba, op. cit., p. 66. Kirk Franklin God's Property. http://members.xoom.com/LyricSource/stomp.txt). Romanus Egudu and Donatus Nwoga, *Igbo Traditional Verse* (London,Ibadan, Nairobi, Heinemann, 1973 p. 15.

52. http://www.ohhla.com/anonymous/brnubian/one_for/ill4one.brn.txt

53.   http://www.ohhla.com/anonymous/brnubian/one_for/ill4one.brn.txt. Brand Nubian in *One For All* (album) and Song- "All For One" refers to Casablanca; Derek X renamed himself Sadat X (after late Egyptian president

Anwar Sadat, who was in fact from Nubia).

54. Chinua Achebe, *A Man of The People* (New York and London, Anchor Press, Doubleday, 1967), p. 1

55. Tupac Shakur, "Dear Moma;" Will Smith, "Daddy Loves You."

56. DMX: Earl Simmons from Yonkers, New York.

57. DMX: CD *It's Dark And Hell Is Hot*. Song: The Convo Earl Simmons from Yonkers, New York.

58. Ibid.

59. Ibid.

60. http://members.spree.com/entertainment/mostwanted/dmx/theconvo. htm

61. DMX, Ruff Riders

62. Nas, N Y State of Mind II

63. DJ Premier, N Y State of Mind II

64. 'The Paper Chase,' The Chorus, Jay Z (Shawn Carter) and Foxy Brown (v. II *The Hard Knock Life*-1998.

65. No Limit is from New Orleans, Lousiana. Southern Rappers, known to have more of social message in their songs, are Outkast and Goody Mob.http://kinghiphop.server101.com/ masterplyrics. html

66. Silkk The Shocker, 'I'm A Soldier.'

67. Ibid.

68. Ibid.

69. Sugar Hill Gang [http://yomama.bus.miami.edu/ ldouglas/house/shill/].

70. Hurby Luv Bug and Play provided the album, concept *Black Magic* produced by Salt. 'Song Expression,' Salt N Pepa and Spinderella. (1986). http://www.execpc.com/ mwildt/blckmgic.html

71. http://www.execpc.com/ mwildt/blckmgic.html

72. Ibid.

73. Queen Latifa and De La Soul Unity. http://musicfinder.yahoo.com/shop? d=p&id=queen latifah&cf=11.

74. Queen Latifa and Monie Love, *All Hall the Queen*, song "Ladies

First."http://www.ohhla.com/anonymous/qlatifah/all_hail/ladies.lah.txt--

75. Lauryn Hill, *The MisEducation of Lauryn Hill*, "To Zion." Examples of African praise poems in Romanus Egudu and Donatus Nwoga, op. cit., pp. 19, 22.

76. Ill Nana, Foxy Brown, Charli Baltimore, Charli's rap. http://members.tripod.com/ agreedoylyrics.

77. Lamont 'Big L' Coleman, *The Big Picture* 'Ebonics,'1999. John Hope Franklin and Alfred A. Moss, *From Slavery To Freedom*, p. 552 for positive and negative views on rap and hip hop culture.

78. Ngugi Wa Thiong'o, *Decolonising the Mind: The Politics of Language in African Literature* (London, James Currey Ltd, Nairobi, Kenya and Portsmouth, New Hampshire, Heinemann, 1986), p. 11.

79. Julius Lester, "The Old King and the New King" in *The Last Tales of Uncle Remus*, as told by J. Lester, and illustrated by Jerry Pinkney (New York, Dial Books, 1994), pp. 22-23.

80. David Haynes, *Retold African American Folktales* (Logan, Iowa, Perfection Learning Corporation, 1997), "Anansi Takes a Ride," pp. 32–38, Anansi (Akan) the role of the trickster,"Anansi an the Turtle." pp. 92-97; "Anansi Falls Into His Own Trap," pp. 100-105

81. Egudu and Nwoga, op. cit., p. 14.

82. See Ngugi, op. cit., pp. 11, 31.

83. Ibid., p. 11. Egudu and Donatus Nwoga, op. cit., p. 14.

84. Danquah, *The Akan Doctrine of God*, p. 44.

85. Lester, "The Snake," op. cit., p. 30, [pp. 28-31]. Ngugi, op. cit., pp. 11, 31.

86. Toni Morrison, *Song of Solomon* (New York, Knopf, New York 1987/1977), pp. 49, 301-303.

87. Romanus Egudu and Donatus Nwoga, op. cit., pp. 7, 10-11.

88. Jacob D. Elder (Tristram P. Coffin, ed.), *Song Games From Trinidad and Tobago*, v. XVI (Delaware, Ohio, Publications of The American Folklore Society, 1965/1961), pp. 99, 100, 107.

90. Ibid.,, p. 47.

91. John McWhorter, *The Word On the Street: Fact and Fable American English* (New York and London, Plenum Trade, 1998), pp. 175, 185, 186. A.J. Verdelle, "Classroom Rap"http://www.thenation.com/issue/970127/0127verd.htm

92. Perry and Delpit, *The Real Ebonics Debate*, p. 150.http://www2. colgates. edu/diw/SOAN244bibs.html and http://www.cal.org/Ebonics/ebfillmo.htm

93. Turner, *Africanisms in Gullah Dialect*, p. 224.

94. Ibid., p. 225.

95. Ibid., p. 225; Majors and Billson, op. cit., pp. 55-57.

96. McWhorter, op. cit.,, pp. 51, 134-135, 172.

97. Ibid., p. 167. 97.

98. Chinua Achebe, A Man of The People, p. xii.

99. Ibid., p. xi.

100. Vjange Hazie, "Chitchat/Chitcha Country Gal A foreign Graduation An Ting," *The West Indian American*, v. VIII, No. 6, Hartford, Connecticut, June 1999, p.14

101. Ibid., p. 13.

102. John McWhorter, op, cit., pp. 42-43.

103. Ibid., pp. 167, 183, 194, 267. Elder, op. cit., p. 48.

104. Ibid. Warner-Lewis, op. cit., p. 53.

105. McWhorter, op. cit., pp. 173, 174.

106. Ibid., p. 174. See Zora Neale Hurston's references to Cudjo [Cudjoe Lewis] and the "original Africans, older than Cudjo, who survived on the slave ship *Clothilde* in Robert E. Hemenway, *Zora Neale Hurston, A Literary Biography* (University of Illinois Press, Urbana, Chicago, IL, 1977/1980), pp. 96, 101, 110, 117. John W. Blassingame, *The Slave Community: Plantation Life In the Antebellum South* (New York, Oxford University Press, 1972, 1979), pp. 332-335. Compiled from Charles J. Montgomery, "Survivors from the Cargo of the Negro Slave Yacht *Wanderer*," *American Anthropologist*, n.s. X (Oct. 1908), 611-23. All notes are Montgomery's; the geographical references are to Africa. The country origin and ethnicity are not indicated in the table.

107. James Hardin, "Rembering [Remembering] Slavery: Ex-Slave Narratives

from the WPA Federal Writers' Project," *Folklife Center News*, American Folklife Center, The Library of Congress, Winter, 1999, v. XXI, No. 1, pp. 7-8.

108. McWhorter, op. cit., p. 173. Kunjufu, op. cit., p. II, 7. Dorothy Curtis, *The Celebration of Kwanzaa* (New York, Vantage Press, 1991), pp. 2-3.

109. "*Adinkra Symbolism*," prepared by Professor Ablade Glover, Artists Alliance Gallery, Omanye House, Accra-Tema Road, Accra, Ghana 1969/1992).

110. "Ndiwo Za Mpiru Wotendera" (Mustard Greens with Peanut Sauce), *Umoja News* (October 1997), p. 8.

111. *Dictionary of Word and Phrase Origins* (New York, New York and Evanston, Illinois, Harper and Row, 1962), 158, 159, 165, 201 and Albert H. Marchwardt, revised by J. L. Dillard, *American English* (New York, Oxford University Press, 1980,), pp. 54, 66.

112. Holloway, ed., *Africanisms In American Culture*, p. xii.

113. Ibid., p. 17.

114. *Dictionary of Word and Phrase Origins*, pp. 158, 159, 165, 201.

115. Ibid., p. 199.

116. "Miss Lucy Has Some Fine Daughters," Jacob D. Elder, op. cit., pp. 89–90. *The American Heritage Dictionary*, p. 91.

117. "Ebonics Not Mentioned in Oakland's Final Report," *Black Issues in Higher Education*, May 29, 1997, vol. 14, No. 7, p. 8.

118. Ibid

119. McWhorter, op. cit., p. 218.

120. *The San Francisco Examiner* (12/20/96) quoted in http://www2.colgates.edu/diw/SOAN244bibs.html and http://www.cal.org/Ebonics/ebfill-mo.htm.

121. Theresa Perry and Lisa Delpit, *The Real Ebonics DebatePower Language, and the Education of African-American Children* (Beacon Press, Boston, 1998), pp. 80, 87.

122. McWhorter, *The Word On The Street*, p. 218. African American

Vernacular English Conference with original papers, September 29-30, 1998, Athens, Georgia http://dir.yahoo.com/ Society_ and_Culture/Cultures _and_Groups/Cultures/ American_.../Ebonics. Carolyn Temple Adger from the Center for Applied Linguistics: http://www.cal.org/ericcll/News/9703 Dialect.html.

123. McWhorter, op. cit., 218.

124. Ibid., pp. 142-143, 146.

125. "Amelia's Song," *The Language You Cry In.*

BIBLIOGRAPHY

BOOKS

Abrahams, Roger D., "Rapping and Capping: Black Talk as Art," in John F. Szwed, ed., *Black America*, New York, Basic Books, 1970.

Achebe, Chinua, *A Man of The People,* New York and London, Anchor Press Doubleday, 1967.

Alleyne M.C., "Linguistic Continuity of Africa in the Caribbean," in H.J. Richards, ed., *Topics in Afro-American Studies*, New York, Black, Academy Press, 1971.

Amadiume, Ifi, *African Matriarchal Foundations, The Case of Igbo Societies,* London, Karnak House, 1987/1995.

Appiah, Kwame Anthony, *In My Father's House: Africa in the Philosophy of Culture.* New York, Oxford University Press, 1992/1993.

Arnett, William S., *The Predynastic Origin of Egyptian Hieroglyphs, Evidence for the Development of Rudimentary Forms of Hieroglyphs in Upper Egypt in the Fourth Millenium B.C.*, Washington, D.C., University Press of America, 1982.

Austin, Allan D., *African Muslims in Antebellum America: Transatlantic Stories and Spiritual Struggles*, New York and London, Routledge Press, 1997.

Barber, John W. [Member of the Connecticut Historical Society], *A History of the Amistad Captives: Being a Circumstantial Account of the Capture of the Spanish Schooner Amistad, By the Africans on Board; Their Voyage, and Capture Near Long Island, New York with Biographical Sketches of Each of the Surviving Africans also, An Account of The Trials Had On Their Case, Before The District and*

Circuit Courts of The United States, For the District of Connecticut. New Haven, Connecticut, E.L. & J.W. Barber, 1840, reprinted in New York, Arno Press, Inc., 1969.

Bekerie, Ayele, *Ethiopic: An African Writing System, Its History and Principles*, Lawrenceville, New Jersey and Asmara, Eritrea, Africa World Press, 1997.

Berry, Mary Frances and Blassingame, John W., *Long Memory: The Black Experience in America*, New York, Oxford University Press, 1982.

Blassingame, John W., *The Slave Community: Plantation Life in the Antebellum South*, New York, Oxford University Press, 1972, 1979.

Blassingame, John W., *Slave Testimony: Letters, Speeches, Interviews, and Autobiographies, 1736-1938*, Baton Rouge, Louisiana, University of Louisiana, 1977.

Blyden, Edward Wilmot, *African Life and Customs*, Baltimore, Maryland, Black Classic Press, 1908.

Boahen, Adu, Ajayi, Jacob F. Ade and Michael Tidy, *Topics In West African History*, Essex, England, Longman Group Limited, 1986.

Chomsky, Noam. *Language and Mind*, New York, Harcourt Brace, Janovich, 1972.

Cooper, James Fenimore, *Santanstoe or The Littlepage Manuscripts: A Tale of The Colony*, originally published in 1845, New York, Hurd and Houghton and Cambridge, Riverside Press, 1872 and Lincoln, Nebraska, University of Nebraska, 1962.

Crowder, Micheal, *West Africa: An Introduction to its History*. London, England, Longman Group Limited, 1977/1988.

Curtin, Philip D., *The Atlantic Slave Trade: A Census*, Madison, Wisconsin, University of Wisconsin Press, 1969.

Curtin, Philip D., *Africa Remembered: Narratives by West Africans from the Era of the Slave Trade*, Madison, Wisconsin, University of Wisconsin, 1967.

Curtis, Dorothy, *The Celebration of Kwanzaa*, New York, Vantage Press, 1991.

Dalby, David, "The African Element in Black English," in Thomas Kochman ed., *Rappin' and Stylin' Out*, Urbana, Illinois, University of Illinois Press, 1972.

Danquah, Joseph Buakye, *The Akan Doctrine of God: A Fragment of Gold Coast Ethics and Religion*, London, England, Frank Cass & Co. Ltd., 1944, 1968.

Davidson, Basil, *Modern Africa A Social & Political History*, London, and New York, Longman, 1983/1992.

Davis, David B., *The Problem of Slavery in Western Culture*, Ithaca, New York, Cornell University Press, 1966.

Delany, Martin R., *The Condition, Elevation, Emigration and Destiny of the Colored People of the United States Politically Considered*, New York, Arno Press, 1968, first published 1852.

De Franz, Anita, "Coming to Cultural and Linguistic Awakening: An African and African American Educational Vision," in Jean Frederickson, ed., *Reclaiming Our Voices: Bilingual Education Critical Pedagogy and Praxis*, Ontario, California, Association for Bilingual Education, 1994.

De Saussure, Ferdinand (Editors Charles Bally and Albert Sechehaye). *Course in General Linguistics*, La Salle, Illinois, Open Court Publishing Company, 1972, 1986 (first published in 1916).

Diamond, Arthur, *Paul Cuffee: Merchant and Abolitionist*, New York, Chelsea House Publishers, 1989.

Dillard, J. L., *Black English: Its History and Usage in the United States*, New York, Random,House, 1972.

Dillard, J. L., *Black Names*, The Hague, Mouton, 1976.

Dillard, J. L., *American Talk: Where Our Words Came From,* New York, Random House, 1976.

Diop, Cheik, Anta, *Parenté Génétique de L'Égyptien Pharaonique Et Des Langues Négro-Africaines*, Dakar-Abidjan, Les Nouvelles Editions Africanes and Universite de Dakar, 1977.

DuBois, W.E.B., *The Souls of Black*, Folk. New York, Bantam Classic Edition 1903/1989.

DuBois, W.E.B., *The Supression of the African Slave Trade to the United States of*

America 1638-1870, New York, Dover Publications, Inc. 1970/1896.

DuBois, W.E.B., *Darkwater: Voices From Within The Veil*, New York, Harcourt, Brace And Howe, 1920.

Douglass, Frederick, *Autobiographies: My Bondage and My Freedom, Narrative of the Life of Frederick Douglass, The Life and Times of Frederick Douglass* (originally published in the 1840s),. New York, The Library of America, 1984.

Duignan, Peter and Gann, L.H., *The United States And Africa: A History*, Cambridge, London, and New York, Cambridge University Press and Hoover Institution, 1984.

Egudu, Romanus and Nwoga, Donatus. *Igbo Traditional Verse*, London, Ibadan, Nigeria, Heinemann, 1973.

Elder, Jacob D., *Song Games from Trinidad and Tobago*, v. XVI., Delaware, Ohio, Publications of the American Folklore Society, 1961, 1965.

Emeagwali-Thomas, Gloria, *African Systems of Science Technology and Art The Nigerian Experience*, London, Karnak House, 1993.

Emerson, Rupert, *Africa and United States Policy*, Englewood Cliffs, New Jersey, Prentice-Hall, 1967.

Equiano, Olaudah, *The Interesting Narrative of the Life of Olaudah Equiano*,(originally published 1789), recent ed. Boston, Massachusetts, Bedford Books of St. Martin's Press, 1995.

Fairservis, Walter A., *The Hierakonpolis Project – Hierakonpolis The Graffiti and the Origins of Egyptian Hieroglyphic Writing*, Poughkeepsie, New York, Vassar College, 1978.

Furro, Broteer [Venture Smith], *A Narrative of the Life and Adventures of Venture A Native of Africa But a Resident Above Sixty Years in the United States of America Related By Himself in the anthology*, New London, 1798 and Middletown, Connecticut, J.S. Stewart, Printer and Bookbinder, 1897, reprinted in Arna Bontemps, ed. *Five Black Lives*, New York, Arno Press, 1969; recent edition, Middletown, Connecticut, Wesleyan University Press,

1988.

Gaulaudet, Thomas H., ed., *A Statement with regard to the Moorish Prince, Abduhl Rahahman*, New York, 1828, Olin Library, Rare Books Collection, Cornell University, Ithaca, New York.

Goss, Linda and Barnes, Marian E., editors, *Talk That Talk: An Anthology of African American Storytelling*, New York, Simon and Schuster/Touchstone, 1989.

Hall, Robert Jr., *Pidgin and Creole Languages*, Ithaca, New York, Cornell University Press, 1966.

Hamilton, Virginia, (illustrated by Leo & Diane Dillon), *Her Stories–African American Folktales, Fairy Tales, and True Tales*, New York, The Blue Sky Press, 1995.

Harris, Sheldon H., *Paul Cuffee: Black America and The African Return*, New York, Simon Schuster, 1972.

Haynes, David, *Retold African American Folktales*, Logan, Iowa, Perfection Learning Corporation, 1997.

Hemenway, Robert, Zora Neale Hurston, *A Literary Biography*, Urbana and Chicago, Illinois, University of Illinois Press, 1977, 1980.

Henry, Charles P., *Ralph J. Bunche: Selected Speeches and Writings*, Ann Arbor, Michigan, University of Michigan Press, 1998/1995.

Herskovits, Melville J., *The Myth of the Negro Past*, Boston, Massachusetts, Beacon Press, 1941/1958/ 1990.

Holloway, J. E., *Africanisms in American Culture*, Bloomington, Indiana, Indiana University Press, 1990.

Holloway, Joseph E., and Winifred K. Vass, *The African Heritage of American English*, Bloomington, Indiana, Indiana University Press, 1993.

Howard, Warren S., *American Slavers and the Federal Law, 1837-1862*, Berkeley, University of California Press, 1963.

Hurston, Zora Neale, *Mules and Men*, (first published 1935, renewed 1963),

Blomington, Indiana: Indiana University Press, 1978.

Jones, Regina, ed., *Handbook of Tests and measurements for the Black Population*, Hampton, Virginia, Cobbs and Henry, 1996.

Kellersberger, Julia Lake, *A Life For the Congo: The Story of Althea Brown Edmiston*, London, Edinburgh, and New York, Fleming H. Revell Company, 1947.
Keppel, Ben, *The Work of Democracy: Ralph Bunche, Kenneth B. Clark, Lorraine Hansberry and the Cultural Politics of Race*, Cambridge, Massachusetts, Harvard University Press, 1995.
Kunjufu, Jawanza, *Hip-Hop vs. MAAT: A Psycho/Social Analysis of Values*, Chicago, Illinois, African American Images, 1993.

Lester, Julius, *The Last Tales of Uncle Remus*, New York, Dial Books, 1994.

Lukas, Anthony, *Common Ground: A Turbulent Decade in the Lives of Three American Families*, New York, Knopf, 1985.

Majors, Richard and Billson, Janet Mancini, *Cool Pose: The Dilemmas of Black Manhood In America*, New York, Lexington Books, 1992.
Mannix, Daniel P. and Cowley, Malcolm, *Black Cargoes: A History of the Atlantic Slave Trade*, 1518-1865, New York, Viking Press, 1962.
Marchwardt, Albert, revised by J. L Dillard, *American English*, New York, Oxford University Press, 1980.
Maxon, Robert, *East Africa: An Introductory History*, Morgantown, West Virginia, West Virginia University Press, 1986.
McWhorter, John, *The Word On the Street, Fact and Fable-American English*, New York/London, Plenum, 1998.
Morrison, Toni, *Song of Solomon*, New York, Alfred A. Knopf, 1977.
Moore, Bai Tamia, *Ebony Dust*, Monrovia, Liberia, Ducor Publishing House,

1962/1976.

Moses, Wilson Jeremiah, *Alexander Crummell: a Study of Civilization and Discontent*, New York: Oxford University Press, 1989.

Nkrumah, Kwame, *Ghana: An Autobiography of Kwame Nkrumah*, New York, International Publishers, 1957/1981.

Obenga, Theophile, *Ancient Egypt and Black Africa: A Student's Handbook for the Study of Ancient Egypt in Philosophy, Linguistics, and Gender Relations*, London, Karnak House, 1992.

Painter, Nell Irvin, *Sojourner Truth: A Life, A Symbol*, New York, Norton, 1996.
Perry, Theresa and Delpit, Lisa, *The Real Ebonics Debates: Power, Language and the Education of African-American Children*, Boston, Massachusetts, Beacon Press, 1998.

Reed, Ishmael, *Mumbo Jumbo, A Novel*, New York, Atheneum/Macmillan Publishing Company, 1972/1988.
Richmond, M.A., ed., *Bid The Vassal Soar: Interpretive Essays on the Life and Poetry of Phillis Wheatley and George Moses Horton*, Washington, D.C., Howard University Press, 1974.
Rowan, Carl T., ed.,. *Dream Makers, Dream Breakers: The World of Justice Thurgood Marshall*, Boston, Massachusetts and London, Little, Brown and Company, 1993.

Saxon, Lyle, comp., *Gumbo: Ya-Ya A Collection of Folktales,* Boston, Massachusetts, Houghton Mifflin Co., 1945.
Smitherman, Geneva, *Talkin andTestifyin: The Language of Black America*, Detroit, Wayne State University Press, 1986.
Spence, J., ed., *Achievement and Achievement Motives*, San Francisco, W. H. Freeman, 1983.

Stuckey, Sterling, *Going Through The Storm: The Influence of African American Art in History*, New York, Oxford University Press, 1994.

Thiong'O, Ngugi Wa, *Decolonising the Mind: The Politics of Language In African Literature*, London, James Currey, Nairobi, Heinemann and Portsmouth, New Hampshire, Heinemann, 1981/1986.
Thiong'O, Ngugi Wa, *Moving The Centre: The Struggle For Cultural Freedoms*, London, James Currey, 1993.
Thomas, T. Ajayi, *Juju Music: A History of An African Popular Music from Nigeria*, Jamaica, New York, The Organization, 1992.
Thornton, John K., *The Kingdom of Kongo Civil War and Transition 1641-1718*, Madison, University of Wisconsin Press, 1983.
Turner, Lorenzo D., *Africanisms in the Gullah Dialect*, Chicago, University of Chicago Press, 1949.

Umeh, John Anenechukwu, *After God Is Dibia: Igbo Cosmology, Healing, Divination and Sacred Science In Nigeria*, v. II, London, Karnak House, 1999.

Van Sertima, Ivan, "African Linguistic and Mythological Structures in the New World" in Rhoda L. Goldstein, ed., *Black Life and Culture in the United States*, New York, Thomas Y. Crowell and Company, 1971.
Vass Kellersberger, Winifred, *The Bantu-speaking Heritage of the United States*, Los Angeles, California, Center for Afro-American Studies, UCLA Press, 1979.

Warner-Lewis, Maureen, *Guinea's Other Suns*, Dover, Massachusetts, The Majority Press, 1991.
Warner-Lewis, Maureen, *Yoruba Songs of Trinidad*, London, Karnak House, 1994.
Waterman, Christopher, *Juju: A Social History and Ethnography of an African Popular Music*, Chicago, Illinois, University of Chicago Press, 1990.

Wiggins, Rosalind Cobb, ed., *Captain Paul Cuffe's Logs and Letters, 1808-1817: A Black Quaker's "Voice from within the Veil,"* Washington, D.C., Howard University Press, 1996.

Williams, Robert L., *Ebonics: The true language of Black Folks*, St. Louis, Missouri, Institute of Black Studies, 1975.

Wood, Peter, *Black Majority*, New York, Knopf, 1974.

GRAPHICS

Glover, Ablade, *Adinkra Symbolism :Prepared by Professor Ablade Glover*, Accra, Ghana, Artists Alliance Gallery, Omanye House, 1969/1992.

DATABASE

David Eltis, Stephen D. Behrendt, David Richardson and Herbert S. Klein, *The Transatlantic Slave Trade, 1527-1867*, A Database Prepared at the W.E.B. DuBois Institute" with data from Joseph Inikori on the British slave trade to 1783-1807 and Svend E. Holsoe on slave trade to the Danish colonies, Harvard University, Cambridge, Massachusetts, April 25-26, 1998.

REFERENCES

Microsoft 2000, Encarta Electronic Encyclopedia.

DICTIONARIES

Abboud, Peter F., Bezirgan, Najm A. Erwin, Wallace M., Khouri, Mounah A., McCarus, Ernest N. and Rammuny, Raji M., *Elementary Standard Arabic*, Part One, Ann Arbor, Michigan, University of Michigan Press, 1975.

American Heritage Dictionary Second College Edition, Boston, Massachusetts, Houghton Mifflin Co., 1982/1985.

Cassidy, F. G. and R.B. LePage, *Dictionary of Jamaican English*, Cambridge University Press, London, Cambridge, and Binghamton, New York, Vail-Ballou Press, Inc., 1967/1980.

Dent, G.R. and Nyembezi, C.L.S., *Scholar's Zulu Dictionary*, Pietermaritzburg, South Africa, Shuter and Shooter, 1969.

Dictionary of Word and Phrase Origins, New York and Evanston, Illinois, Harper and Row, 1962.

Doke, Z.C.M., Vilakazt, M.A., D.L.H. and B.W. Vilakazt, *Zulu English Dictionary*, Johannesburg, South Africa, Witwatersrand University Press, 1948.

Gailey, Harry, *A. Historical Dictionary of Gambia*, Metuchen, New Jersey and London, Scarecrow Press Inc., 1987.

Fashagba, Joseph Ajayi, *The First illustrated Yoruba Dictionary, Two Parts: Yoruba-English, English-Yoruba*, Toronto, Canada, 1991.

Greenberg, Joseph, *The Languages of Africa*, Bloomington, Indiana University Press, 1963.

Hodge, Carleton T. and Umaru,Ibrahim,. *Hausa Basic Course*, Washington, D.C., Foreign Service, Institute, 1963.

Major, Clarence, ed., *Black Slang A Dictionary of Afro-American Talk*, London, Routledge and Kegan Paul, 1971.

Major, Clarence, ed., *Juba to Jive, A Dictionary of African-American Slang*, New York, Penguin Books, 1970/1994.

Mataranyika, Matthew, Stevick, Earl W. and Cordova, Gabriel, *Shona Basic Course*, Washington, D.C., Foreign Service Institute, Department of State, 1965.

Mufwene, Salikoko S, ed., *Africanisms in Afro-American Language Varieties*, Athens, Georgia, University of Georgia Press, 1993.

Obolesnsky, Serge, Zelelie, Debebow and Andualem, Mulugeta, *Amharic Basic Course*, Units 51-60, Reader Glossary, Washington, D.C., Foreign Service

Institute, 1965.

Osepetetreku, Kwame Osei, *The Ancient Egyptian Origins of The English Language*, Accra, New Town, Ghana and Brooklyn, New York, Trans Atlantic International and Camden Graphics, 1996.

Shipley, Joseph T., *The Origins of English Words: A Discussive Dictionary of Indo-European Roots*, Baltimore, Maryland and London, Johns Hopkins University Press, 1984.

Stevick, Earl W., Aremu, Olayeye, Simaren, Josiah , Edwards, Alexander and Adebonojo, Samuel, *Yoruba Basic Course*, Washington, D.C., Foreign Service Institute, 1963.

Stevick, Earl W. and Kamoga, Frederick Katabazi (Series editor Augustus A. Koski), *Luganda Pretraining Program*, Washington, D.C., Foreign Service Institute, 1970.

Swift, Lloyd, Ahaghota, Amako and Ugorji, Chidiadi, *Igbo Basic Course*, Washington, D.C., Foreign Service Institute, Department of State, 1962.

Swift, Lloyd B., Tambad, Kalilu, and Imhoff, Paul G., *Fula Basic Course*, Washington, D.C., Foreign Service Institute, 1965.

Tourneux, Henry and Barbotin, Maurice, *Dictionnaire Pratique du Creole de Guadelope suivi d'un index Francais-Creole*, Paris, France, Karthala–ACCT, Marie-Galante, 1990.

Traore, O. and W. A. Stewart, *Notes on Wolof Grammar*, Dakar, Senegal, unpublished copy.

Zawawi, Sharifa M. Onegea, *Converse Kiswahili*, Trenton, New Jersey, Africa World Press, 1991.

FEDERAL BILINGUAL EDUCATION ACT AND EBONICS RESOLUTION
Federal Bilingual Education Act (20 U.S.C. 1402 et seq.), in "Ebonics Not Mentioned in Oakland's Final Report," *Black Issues In Higher Education*, May 29, 1997, vol. 14, No. 7, p. 8.

"Oakland Amends Ebonics Resolution," *Black Issues in Higher Education*, vol.

13, No. 25, February 6, 1997, p. 29-31. Full text of resolution pp. 24-25.

MAPS AND GUIDE BOOKS

Caribbean including the Bahamas and Bermuda Travel Book, Heathrow, Florida, American Automobile Association, 1994.

Europa World Year Book 1997, v. I, Part One: *International Organizations*; Part Two, London, Europa Publications Limited, 1926/1997.

Georgia and Alabama Map, Heathrow, Florida, American Automobile Association, 1993.

Keown, Ian M., *Guide To The Dutch Caribbean*, New York, KLM Royal Dutch Airlines, 1972/1975.

Rand McNally Road Atlas, United States/Canada/Mexico, New York and Chicago, Rand McNally & Company, 1978.

Smallwood, Arwin with Elliot, Jeffrey M., *The Atlas of African-American History and Politics from The Slave Trade To Modern Times*, Boston, Massachusetts and New York, McGraw Hill, 1998.

Southeastern States Map, Heathrow, Florida, American Automobile Association, 1998.

ARTICLES

American Legacy, Winter 1998, v. 4/No.4, pp. 33, "America's First Black Muslims," Winter 1998, v.4/No.4.

Burrowes, Carl Patrick, "Some Structures of Everyday Life in Pre-Liberian Coastal Societies, 1660-1747," *Liberia Studies Journal*, v. XVIII 1993, No.2.

Dunlap, David W. and Cronin, Anne, "A Black Cemetery Takes Its Place in History," The New York Times, Sunday, February 28, 1993, p. E5.

Ebenezer, E. Keto, translated by L. Krasean, "Boundaries of Yesterday, Borders of Today and.Tomorrow," *Afrique Histoire*, No. 1, 1982.

"'Ebonics' Not Mentioned in Oakland's Final Report," *Black Issues In Higher*

Education, May 29, 1997, vol. 14, No. 7, p. 8

Fields, Cheryl D., "Histrionics About Ebonics Ebonics 101 – What Have We Learned," *Black Issues in Higher Education*, January 23, 1997, vol. 13, No. 24.

Hall, Perry A., "Introducing African American Studies Systematic and Thematic Principles," *Journal of Black Studies*, vol. 26, No. 6, July 1996.

Hazie. Vjange, "Chitchat/Chitcha Country Gal A Foreign Graduation An Ting," *The West Indian American*, v. VIII, No. 6, Hartford, Ct, June 1999.

Hazie. Vjange, "Chitchat- Country Gal A Foreign," The West Indian American, v. VIII, No. 5, May 1999.

Manfredi, Victor. "Sourcing African English in North America," *International Journal of African Historical Studies*, Boston, Massachusetts, Boston University Press, 1995/1996.

Manzo, Kathleen Kenned, "Dr. William L. Blakey and Unearthing the African American Past," *Black Issues in Higher Education*, April 21, 1994, v. 11, No. 4.

Muyumba, François N, "Music and Power in Contemporary Africa: Language and Expressivity," *The Literary Griot*, 5, 1, Spring 1993.

Moore, Bai Tamia, "Problems of Vai Identity in terms of My Own Experience," *Liberian Studies Journal*, v. XV, 2, 19902.

"Ndiwo Za Mpiru Wotendera" (Mustard Greens with Peanut Sauce), *Umoja News*, (October 1997).

"Oakland Amends Ebonics Resolution," *Black Issues in Higher Education*, vol. 13, No. 25, February 6, 1997. Full text of resolution pp. 24-25].

Ofri-Scheps, Dorith, "Bai T. Moore's Poetry and Liberian Identity: An Offering To The Ancestors," *Liberian Studies Journal*, v. XI, No.2, *Liberian Studies Journal*, v. XV, No. 2 (1990).

Perry, Warren R. "Analysis of the African Burial Ground Archaeological Materials," *Update Newsletter of the African Burial Ground & Five Points Archeological Projects* (February/March 1997), vol. 2, No. 2.

Peters, Pearlie, "Women and Assertive Voice in Hurston's Fiction and Folklore," *The Literary Griot*, vol. 4, Nos. 1 & 2, Spring/Fall 1992.

Pierce, Jade Pierce, "Ev'y Bodies Talkin' 'Bout Black English: Ebonics," *The Vision*, vol 17, No. 23, University of Connecticut, H. Fred Simmons African American Cultural Center, March , 1997 (Storrs, Connecticut).

Reed, Allen W., "The Speech of Negroes in Colonial America," *Journal of Negro History*, v. XXIV (1939).

Reddick, III, Rev. Lawrence L, "On Youth Currents Beneath The Ebonics Debate," *The Christian Journal*, Feb.,1997, Hartford, CT.

Rickford, John R., "Suite For Ebony and Phonics," *Discover*, December 1997.

Ross, Randy, "Beyond Ebonics" and "Why 'Black English' Matters," *Education Week*, January 29.

Steele, Shelby, "Indoctrination Isn't Teaching," *Education Week*, January 29, 1997.

Stone, Ruth, "Indigenous Invention: The Indigenous Kpelle Script in the Late Twentieth Century," *Liberian Studies Journal*, v. XV, (1990).

Twe, Boakai S., "Edward W. Blyden's Lessons in African Psychology," *Liberian Studies Journal*, v. XXI,(1996).

White, David O., "Augustus Washington, Black Daguerrreotypist of Hartford," *The Connecticut Historical Society Bulletin* (January 1974), v. 39, No. 1.

Wilkie, Rubie, "Rap Music," *The AFRIKAN*, 2nd Issue 1996-1997.

SPEECH

Hugh B. Price, President, National Urban League, February 14, 1997, "The 'No Excuses' Era of Urban School Reform," p. 1.

FILM

Dash, Julie. "Daughters of The Dust," Geechee Girls Production, 1991.

"Indians of North America Series – Seminole," Invision Comm Inc., Schlesinger Video Productions Division, Bala Cynwya, Pennsylvania, 1993.

Toepke, Alvaro, Serrano, Angel (producer/director),with Grosvernor, Vertamae, narrator, "The Language You Cry in: The Story of a Mende Song," Sierra Leone/Spain, California Newsreel Distributors, 1998.

PAMPHLET

Fayomi, Ogundipe, *Layout and Illustration Afrikan Names, Why, Which, What Where*, Brooklyn, New York, East Distribution and Publication, 1974.

INTERNET

"Meanings of Symbols In Adinkra Cloth," Kwaku Ofori Ansa (oana@cldc.howard.edu).   Web page created by Kwadwo Boahene. jtt://www.erols.com/kemet/adinkra.htm. 1/29/98.

Mojo http:/1www.sonic.net/% 7Eyronwode mojo.html Jim Morrison "Mojo rising." My Mojo Risin," Muddy Waters (McKinley Morganfield) www.yomama. bus. miami.edu/ldouglas/house/shill/

http://www.diryahoo.com/Society_and_Culture/Cultures_and_Groups/Cultu res/American_.../Ebonics Morgan "Ain't nothin' but a G thang': Grammar, variation and language ideology in hip hop identity";

Salikoko "What is African-American English?"   Original papers from the African American Vernacular English Conference, September 29-30, Athens, Georgia.

www. thenation.com/issue/970127/0127verd.htm A. J. Verdelle, "Classroom Rap."

www2.colgates.edu/diw/SOAN244bibs.html

www.cal.org/Ebonics/ebfillmo.htm.

www.members.xoom.com/LyricSource/stomp.txt

www.execpc.com/mwildt/blckmgic.html

www.newsreel.org/films/langyou.htm

www.mrblunt.com/culture/hh_net.html

www.whudat.com/tags.html
www,calarg/ericcll/News/9703 Dialect.html
http://www.stanford.edu./-rickford/
http://musicfinder. Yahoo.com/shop?dp&id=queentalifah&=11
http://www,ohhla.com/anonymous/qlatifah/all_hail/ladieslah.txt
http://members.tripodcom./agree.daylyrics
http://kinghiphop.server101.com/masterplyrics.html
http://members.spreecom/entertainment/most wanteddmx/theconvo.htm
http://www.ohhla.com/anonymous/brnubian/one-for/1140ne
http://wwwnet.fi/users/llcooj/wannahurtmase.htm
http://publicenemy.com/archives/lyrics/index.html
www.webcom.com/-duane/truth.html
www.lkwdpl.org/wihohio/trut-soj.htm

COMPACT DISCS AND RECORDINGS
Coleman, 'Big L' Lamont, *The Big Picture* (1999)
Hill, Lauren, *The Miseducation of Lauren Hill* (1999).
Simmons, DMX Earl, *It's Dark And Hell Is Hot*, (1998).
Slick Rick , *The Art of Storytelling* (1999).
Shakur, Tupac, 'Dear Mama' (1996).
The Sugar Hill Gang vs. Grandmaster Flash & The Furious Five, *The Showdown* (1999).

INDEX

Abantu (Bantu) 16, 24, 39, 42

Achebe, Chinua 85

Adissa 54

Adinkra 16-18, 90

African American

    Burial Site 18, 24

    Children 6-9, 92

    Folktales

    Language Systems 9

    Linguistic formations 11

    Speech 8, 21, 114

    Vernacular English 120-121

African languages 8, 16-24

African proverbs 42, 90

African writing scripts 17, 26

Akan 13, 15-18, 25-27, 29-30, 32, 35-43

Akimbo 91

Amarigna (Amharic) 18

Arabic 13, 18-16, 19-20, 28, 32, 80, 87, 90

Baluba 13, 15

bell hooks 83

Benin 13, 57, 86

Bi-dialecticalism 93

Binary repetition 63, 71

Black English 9, 81, 83, 85-87, 89-91

Bunche, Ralph 12, 21-25, 34

California State Legislature 9

Cameroon 13-14, 22, 55, 77

    Bamileke in Cameroon 15

Caribbean Africanized English 86

Caribbean patois 86-87

Cape Verdian Crioulo 14, 40

Center for Applied Linguistics 12, 120

Chinese 90

Choctaw 43, 91

Code switching 55-56

College students and Ebonics 92

Congolese Kiswahili 89

Cook, Toni Note # I Chapter I

Covey, James Kaw-we-li 19

Creek (Seminole – Siminoli) 41

Danish 11

Database on the slave trade, W.E.B. DuBois Institute at Harvard University (Cambridge, Massachusetts) 14

Delany, Martin 20

Delpit, Lisa 6

Dey 20

Dialect 9, 10

Dialect readers 12

Diachronic linguistics 8

Diaspora 46, 53, 59, 62, 78, 80-87

Dirge 60-62, 67, 70
Douglass, Frederick 20- 21, 90
DuBois, William Edward Burkhardt
11, 13, 23
Dutch 11, 21, 23, 29, 90

Ebonics 6-14, 21, 48, 83, 87-90, 93
Egyptian 8, 17, 52, 89
Egyptian Arabic 93
Elder, J. D.   82-83,87-88
Elliptical juxtapositions 52
English 6, 8-11, 18-20, 24-25, 27, 32-42,
46, 48, 53, 59, 76-77, 81-86, 88-91
English Creole 85
Equiano, Olaudah (Gustavas Vassa)
18-19
Ethnic 13-14
Ewondo 36
Expressive oral and aural traditions
47 ,50-51

Federal Binlingual Education Act 9
Federal Writers Project Administra-
tion 88
French 11, 13, 53, 85, 90
French Creole 87
Fon 87
Fulani, Fulbe 13, 20
Folklore 44-45, 79

Gaye, Marvin 9

Gechee 25-30, 34, 76, 82
German 11-14, 17, 86
Ghana 11-14, 17, 86
Gikuyu 14, 25, 79
Gola 20, 20, 28, 30, 57, 60
Griot 30, 57, 60, 77
Graffiti 54
Grammar 6, 9, 16, 33, 35, 46-47, 64,
83-84, 88, 90-91
Guinea 13-14, 20
Gullah, Geechee 22, 25-30, 34, 36, 42,
76-84, 142

Hausa 13-14, 16, 27, 28-32, 87
Herskovits, Melville 11
Hieroglyphs 16, 25, 41, 54
Hip Hop 45, 47-48, 50-55, 78
Hughes, Langston 11

Igbo (Ibo) 16, 19, 27-29, 38, 40, 62,
64, 79, 82, 86
Ibrahima, Abd-ar Rahman 20
Italian 54, 90

Jamaica 45

Kasala 57, 60, 64
Kikongo 87
Kissi 28
Kiswahili 15, 17, 24, 55, 89-90, 93
Kwanzaa 89, 92

Language 6-12, 13-20, 25, 27-32, 35-37, 40-44, 55, 59, 61-62, 78-79, 83-92
Lexical juxtaposition 73
Liberia 13, 28
Linguistics 6-8, 10-12, 14-20, 24-25, 30-32, 45-46, 61, 83, 85-87, 89, 93
Lingala 50, 55
Luba 16
Luganda 16

Maat 89, 92
Madagascar 16
Mali 13, 16, 57
Malinke 13, 29
Mandinka 13, 20, 28-29, 33, 36, 41, 84-85
Marshall, Thurgood 24
Mashona 16
McWhorter, John 83, 85, 87-88, 93
Men 11, 32, 47, 58-59
Mende (Mendi) 13, 19-20, 29, 32, 35, 93
Muslim Africans 18, 20, 28

Nana 27, 30, 34, 48, 77
Niger-Congo Rivers confluence 7, 14, 16, 19, 85
Nigeria 13, 17, 21, 30, 66, 85
Nkrumah, Kwame 11, 12
North African School (Hartford, Connecticut) 9

Nyame 28, 34, 64

Oakland Unified School District 6-7, 12, 91 (officials), 91-92 (Board)
Oware 89

Pan African linguistic heritage 7, 12 (language), 12, 93; (comm. patterns) 83
Behaviors 6, 9
Papiamento 31
Pepe Kale Mua 55
Perry, Theresa 6, 92
Pinkster 22-23
Portuguese 11, 42
Praise song 55, 64, 66-67, 75-76

Rap 47-55, 57-62, 64-66, 68-78, 83, 93

Sankofa 18
Secret, Carrie 92
Senegal 13-14, 17, 21, 57
Seminole (Siminoli) 41
Sierra Leone 13-14, 19, 22, 29, 36, 48, 93
Sing-gbe Pieh 19
Slang 7-9, 38
Slave trade 12, 14, 16, 23-24, 29, 40, 61, 89
Smith, Ernie A. 10, 83
Song games 47, 78, 81-83

Spanish 11, 87
Sranan 86-87
Standard English Proficiency Program 91-93
Synchronic 7, 28-30, 45
Syntax 7, 17, 93

Temne 13, 22, 29, 36
Trinidad 20, 31, 35, 38, 61-62, 82, 87
Turner, Lorenzo 28-30, 34, 37, 84
Twi 29, 35, 38-39, 86

Vai 17-19, 29, 32, 36
Vocabulary 7, 17, 25, 40-41, 78, 89, 93

Warner-Lewis, Maureen 31, 61-63, 87
Wheatley, Phillis 20
Williams, Robert L. 10, 23
Wolof 13, 17-18, 20, 29, 33-35, 37-38, 43, 90-91
Women 10-11, 60, 64, 73-74, 88

Yoruba 13, 15-16, 19-20, 27, 29, 31, 35-36, 44, 61-64, 66, 82, 86-88, 91

Zaire 13, 16, 48
Zimbabwe 48